PSYCHOLOGY OF LEARNING

£3.55

PSYCHOLOGY OF LEARNING:
Educational Applications

JAMES M. ROYER, Ph.D.
Associate Professor of Psychology and Education
Department of Psychology
University of Massachusetts
Amherst, Massachusetts

RICHARD G. ALLAN, Ed.D.
Vice President for Instructional Development
National Evaluation Systems
Amherst, Massachusetts

John Wiley & Sons, Inc., Publishers
New York • Santa Barbara • London • Sydney • Toronto

Publisher: Judy V. Wilson
Editor: Irene Brownstone
Production Manager: Ken Burke
Copyeditor: Gail Larrick
Artist: Douglas Luna
Compositor: Grace Harwood

100761

Library of Congress Cataloging in Publication Data

Royer, James M.   1941-
    Psychology of learning.

    (Wiley self-teaching guides)
    Includes index.
    1.   Learning, Psychology of.   I.   Allan, Richard G.,
1943-   joint author.   II.   Title.
LB1051.R69   370.15'2   77-12390
√ ISBN 0-471-02270-5
        0108739
Printed in the United States of America

78 79 10 9 8 7 6 5 4 3 2 1

154.4
ROY

DEDICATION

To Marge Doty and Yvonne Allan

ACKNOWLEDGEMENTS

A number of people have been important in the production of this book. First and perhaps foremost we owe a debt of gratitude to Irene Brownstone, our editor at John Wiley & Sons, whose editorial talents have contributed enormously to the comprehensibility of this book. In addition we are grateful to Judy Wilson, the publisher of the Self-Teaching Guides series, for remaining patient over a long development period.

    We would also like to thank Glenn Allan whose help with programming came at a critical time. And finally we would like to thank our wives, Paula and Carol, who provided encouragement and assistance when it was needed.

To the Reader

This book is designed to teach you how to put theories of learning to practical use. Learning has always been a fascinating psychological topic. Virtually all organisms can learn—that is, they have the capability to permanently change their behavior patterns after exposure to some environmental event. Humans are particularly adept at learning. If the contents of the average adult's memory were written in book form, a very respectable library would result!

Because learning is so central to understanding behavior, psychologists have devoted considerable attention to developing theories of learning. If you have ever taken a course in psychology, or read a book about psychology, you have probably come into contact with one or more learning theories.

However, most of these books emphasize the theoretical and scientific aspects of learning. A person interested in doing something practical with learning theory (such as applying it in the classroom) is given little or no guidance in how to do that.

This book was written to help people overcome that problem. Rather than emphasizing the theories of learning, we have focused on the applications of learning theory. We have set our examples in the classroom, since that is where enormous amounts of critical learning occurs. However, these applications are appropriate to <u>any</u> situation that involves learning. In this book we will discuss the basics of three major learning theories and will present step-by-step procedures for transforming these theories into practical solutions to classroom problems. We will also give you considerable practice in using these procedures, so that you can apply them directly and immediately to the classroom—or to any learning situation.

How to Use This Book

This is a self-instructional book. As such, it is organized differently than a traditional text. Each chapter begins with a series of objectives. The objectives state what you can expect to learn by the time you finish the chapter. The chapters then conclude with Self-Tests directly related to the objectives, which allow you to assess your learning.

A Self-Teaching Guide uses an interactive process. Rather than just presenting information, we ask you to use that information to analyze situations, to plan how you might use the information in your classroom, or to test your memory. Questions are interspersed throughout the chapters. The answer for each question is provided below the line of dashes right after the question so you can see how well you are learning the material. Each Self-Test is also followed immediately by the answers so you can check your progress.

Chapter 7 is designed to be a bridge between the information provided in the book and personal application of the learning theories in your own classroom or learning situation. If you are able to answer the chapter Self-Test questions and satisfactorily complete Chapter 7, you should be able to apply the learning theories presented.

Contents

Introduction

Assume that you have recently graduated from college and have been certified as a teacher. You have just been hired by a local school system. On the first day of school, you wander into the teachers' lounge. At the table next to you, several teachers who seem to have quite a bit of experience are engaged in a conversation, which goes something like this:

Ms. Jones:	"That Billy Smith is going to drive me crazy!"
Mr. Johnson:	"Why?"
Ms. Jones:	"Every time I start to talk, he sneezes, and the whole class laughs. When I stop to yell at him, I lose my train of thought. I begin over, and he sneezes again. Claims he's allergic to something in the classroom."
Mr. Johnson:	"My, my. That does sound difficult."
Ms. Simpson:	"Well, let me tell you about my students, particularly that Janie Brainchild. I don't have any discipline problems, but I'm still concerned. As you know, I have the best students in the school, but they don't study enough! I pile on the

work and tell them to read it all, but they don't finish. What can I do? Each day in class, I wind up reviewing the previous night's assignment. "

Mr. Carter: "This discipline and academic concern is all very well, but I have something more serious to consider. Some of my students are social outcasts. They very seldom speak to me or to the other children in the class, and they are most uncooperative. "

After leaving the teachers' lounge, as you are walking down the hall, you happen to hear two students talking:

Billy Smith: "Boy, have I got old Jones on the run. Every time she starts to say something, I sneeze. Then she gets off the track and gets in only half of the lesson. It works every time. "

Janie Brainchild: "Yeah, we figured out Ms. Simpson, too. If we don't do our homework, she reviews it all in class the next day. What about those kids in Mr. Carter's class, though? My sister has him, and she's worried about some of her classmates. "

Billy Smith: "I'm worried, too. Some of those kids are really out of it. I wish they could get some help. "

Over the next few days, you think about the two conversations you over-heard and about some of the other situations you have encountered in your new school. Apparently, some of the students are more successful in controlling the behavior of their teachers than the teachers are in controlling the behavior of their students. Obviously, some of the tactics the teachers are using—such as yelling, punishment, and extra homework—are not working very well.

In thinking about problems that other teachers are having, you begin to consider some of your own problems. In particular, you are very concerned about two of the students in your class. George is a well-behaved boy who transferred from a school where, for some reason, he had never learned how to do arithmetic. As a result, George is well behind the rest of the children in the class, even though he works very hard on his lessons. You simply do not have the time to tutor George individually, and you are concerned that if George does not catch up soon, he will get discouraged and quit trying.

Mary, who is also in your class, has a very different problem. She is so far ahead of the rest of the class that she is getting bored. You know that Mary is very interested in entomology and wants to study and make a collection of all the varieties of mosquitoes that live in the area. The problem is that Mary does not have the skills necessary to classify the different mosquito types. You know that if Mary doesn't become involved soon, she, too, will lose interest in school.

In a conversation with Bernie Richards, one of your fellow teachers, you discover another kind of problem. As Bernie teaches a section on geology in his science class, he is becoming concerned that his students are simply memorizing things without gaining any real understanding of the material or any ability to apply it meaningfully. For example, after two weeks of class work on the factors producing earthquakes and the most likely sites for earth-quakes in the United States, Bernie gave his students a map of the world and asked them to guess probable sites for earthquakes. To his dismay, the students seemed to pick locations almost at random. They showed no ability to apply or generalize the "facts" they had learned.

The problems that you, the hypothetical new teacher, have encountered in your new job are not at all unique. All teachers encounter similar problems. Both new and experienced teachers often feel considerable dismay when facing such problems, because they are not equipped with the "tools" they need to analyze these problems and to develop techniques for dealing with them. The purpose of this book is to acquaint you with some procedures, based on major theories of learning, which have proven useful in dealing with the kinds of problems described above. In addition, the book will give you practice in applying these procedures to problem situations similar to those you may encounter in your own classroom.

Note that the kinds of problems described above can be classified into three types:

1. Problems involving observable student behaviors. Several problems mentioned above involve students who, through their behaviors, com-pletely disrupted normal classroom activities. Billy Smith and Janie Brainchild, for example, through their sneezing and off-the-track questions, disrupted the class to the point where little important

learning was occurring. Other problems falling into this category are characterized by an absence of certain kinds of observable behavior. For example, the children that Billy and Janie mentioned in their conversation might be students who are withdrawn and who rarely engage in social interactions either inside or outside the classroom.

2. <u>Problems involving lack of critical skills.</u> George, the student mentioned above, has a problem which exemplifies this type. Students who are deficient in critical basic skills such as reading proficiency or computational ability are left behind by their classmates and frequently lose all interest in school. Mary's problem, which is different from George's, also falls into this category. Her problem is that she wants to progress beyond many of her classmates, but she lacks the skills to do so. Like George, she could easily become bored and frustrated in school and lose interest.

3. <u>Problems associated with lack of conceptual understanding.</u> Bernie Richards has a problem which falls into this category. His students seem to master facts satisfactorily but cannot apply those facts to new situations. The ability to apply learned information to new situations is a critical test of whether or not the information has been understood. Most teachers are adept at presenting facts to students but have more difficulty in presenting information so that students grasp the concepts behind the facts.

This book will present three theories of learning which have evolved from the science of psychology. No one theory is more correct than another. Rather, each of the three theories seems to be uniquely suited for dealing with a different type of educational problem.

Chapters 1 and 2 present and give you practice in using Operant Learning Theory. Operant Learning Theory has proven to be very useful in dealing with problems involving observable student behaviors. The methods of analysis and the techniques associated with Operant Learning Theory have been successfully applied to problems ranging from severe discipline problems to lack of social interaction.

Chapters 3 and 4 are concerned with Associative Learning Theory, which provides a method for breaking down complex skills into subskills. Associative Learning Theory also provides procedures for presenting these skills so that satisfactory learning of the skills is attained. It is particularly useful in dealing with problems involving the lack of critical skills.

Chapters 5 and 6 present the basic concepts and educational applications of Cognitive Learning Theory. Cognitive Learning Theory is concerned with the ways in which knowledge is acquired; it is mostly applicable in situations involving lack of conceptual understanding. This theory provides some guidelines for presenting information in classrooms so that students are much more likely to understand it, rather than simply to memorize it.

Chapter 7 reviews the three theories in an integrated framework and presents case studies which demonstrate how the theories can be applied in actual classroom situations.

PART ONE
Operant Learning Theory

CHAPTER ONE
Principles of Operant Learning Theory for Classroom Use

Operant Learning Theory serves as a tool which can be applied to modify certain kinds of student behaviors. The teaching technique evolving from the theory involves the systematic use of reward and punishment (1) to decrease the incidence of undesirable student behaviors and (2) to increase the incidence of desirable student behaviors. The ultimate intention of the technique is to replace disruptive or undesirable behaviors with positive and beneficial behaviors. This task is accomplished by systematically rewarding (and thus reinforcing) positive behaviors and systematically withholding reward for (and thus punishing) negative behaviors. Providing reward following a behavior increases the frequency of occurrence of that behavior, whereas systematically withholding reward or providing punishment following a behavior decreases the frequency of the behavior. The theory was developed primarily by Dr. B. F. Skinner and grew out of Skinner's work with animals in laboratory settings.

Chapter 1 presents the teaching goals and principles which have evolved during application of Operant Learning Theory to real-life situations. The chapter is divided into three sections. The first section concerns the purposes of applied Operant Learning Theory and defines the specific kinds of situations in which Operant Learning Theory might be applied. The second section discusses the basic principles of Operant Learning Theory and issues with regard to its application. The third section describes how one can actually apply these principles to appropriate situations.

After completing this chapter, you should be able to:

1. Specify the general type of situation in which the application of Operant Learning Theory should be useful.
2. Specify the principles upon which Operant Learning Theory is based.
3. Identify situations where social reinforcement is appropriate or inappropriate.
4. Identify situations where token economies are appropriate or inappropriate.
5. Identify situations where punishment combined with reward is appropriate or inappropriate.

Later, we'll discuss some of the controversial issues involved in the application of Operant Learning Theory. First, let's determine what Operant Learning Theory is.

PURPOSES OF APPLIED OPERANT LEARNING THEORY

The general purpose of applied Operant Learning Theory is to modify student behaviors in certain kinds of situations. Those situations where Operant Learning Theory might be appropriately applied reflect two characteristics:

1. Normal procedures for dealing with student problems do not work.
2. The problem in question involves an observable student behavior.

Let's look at the first of these characteristics in greater depth. Operant Learning Theory should be formally applied only where normal procedures have been tried and have failed. Thus (1) the problem in question must have existed for some time, and (2) other procedures should have been tried before one decides to apply techniques based on Operant Learning Theory.

1. Ms. Smith has been teaching her second grade class for nearly a week. One of her students, Hannah Horrible, has managed each day to disrupt the class. Hannah's favorite trick, among others, is to pour glue in the hair of the boy who sits in front of her. Should Ms. Smith apply Operant Learning Theory to Hannah's behavior? Why or why not?

   _____

   _____

   _____

   _____

- -

No. Hannah's problem does not have a known long history (it may be transitory), and Ms. Smith should first try other ways of dealing with Hannah.

2. We have said that Operant Learning Theory should be applied formally only where the problem has a long history and other procedures have been tried and have failed. Does this limitation mean that teachers should use reward and punishment only in these situations?

   _____

   _____

   _____

- - - - - - - - - - - - - - - - - -

Certainly not. Teachers should make ample use of reward, particularly in the form of verbal encouragement, at all times. Punishment is a more complex issue to be discussed extensively in a later section of this chapter.

The second characteristic of situations where Operant Learning Theory might appropriately be used is that the problem must involve an observable student behavior. Problems such as disruptive classroom behavior, poor work and study habits, withdrawal from social interactions, and aggressive or abusive behavior fall into the category of observable student behaviors. In theory, any behavior problem that can be observed could be modified through the use of techniques based on Operant Learning Theory. However, teachers should be very careful to choose to modify only those behaviors which inhibit the learning process. For instance, an exuberant student whose outbursts are infrequent, minimally disruptive, and related to the topic being discussed should not necessarily be the target of Operant Learning Theory. However, if the outbursts are frequent and disruptive and the student has not been responsive to other procedures, then Operant Learning Theory might be appropriately applied.

Recognition of the kinds of "problem behavior" which are observable and therefore appropriate for application of Operant Learning Theory is important.

3.   Which of the following are observable behaviors?

_____ a.   John makes frequent outbursts in class.

_____ b.   Sam is not learning enough.

_____ c.   Billy sneezes repeatedly in class, though he is not ill.

_____ d.   You have a feeling that some of your students don't like your subject.

_____ e.   The class does not pay attention when you are ready to begin the lesson.

_____ f.   Students do not come to class with their homework finished and ready to pass in.

_____ g.   Judy is not learning as much math as she should.

_____ h.   Joe never has a friendly discussion with anyone in the class.

- - - - - - - - - - - - - - - - - -

Items a, c, e, f, h are observable behaviors. Items b, d, and g are difficult to observe. You must isolate a particular behavior if you wish to modify it. For instance, Billy's sneezing is obvious to everyone around him and distracts from the learning process in class. His behavior is (1) observable and (2) a detriment to learning; it is therefore, worthy of modification.

In the overview to this chapter, we indicated that applied Operant Learning Theory had a dual purpose: (1) to reduce the incidence of disruptive or undesirable behaviors and (2) to increase the incidence of positive and beneficial behaviors. Thus, in most situations involving Operant Learning Theory, both desirable and undesirable behaviors are the targets of modification techniques. The logic involved in selecting both desirable and undesirable behaviors for modification is that a student who is engaged in appropriate activity can't at the same time be behaving inappropriately. The attempt is made, then, to supplant undesirable behaviors with desirable ones.

The following exercises will give you some practice in identifying behaviors to encourage (increase in frequency) and behaviors to discourage (decrease in frequency). For each situation, list at least two specific behaviors to encourage and two specific behaviors to discourage.

4. Billy Smith sneezes in class virtually every time the teacher begins to talk, although he is not ill. Many students in the class laugh when Billy sneezes, with the result that the class is completely disrupted.

    Behaviors to discourage: _____

    _____

    _____

    Behaviors to encourage: _____

    _____

    _____

- - - - - - - - - - - - - - - - - - - -

Behaviors to discourage: The most obvious behavior to discourage is Billy's sneezing. The class might also be discouraged from laughing at Billy, with two probable results. First, the class would be disrupted less. Second, since Billy is likely to be sneezing to gain class attention, if class attention is withheld, Billy may stop sneezing.

Behaviors to encourage: Encourage Billy to take positive actions, (for example, to be attentive, to work quietly, to raise his hand). Encourage the class to be attentive and to ignore Billy when he sneezes.

5. Janie Brainchild is a bright young woman, but she has miserable study habits. During study periods she plays the role of social butterfly, moving from student to student. Thus she generally disrupts the study habits of everyone else.

   Behaviors to discourage: _____

   _____

   _____

   Behavior to encourage: _____

   _____

   _____

- - - - - - - - - - - - - - - - - -

   Behavior to discourage: Discourage Janie's flitting behavior during study periods. Discourage other students from attending to Janie when she approaches them during study periods.

   Behavior to encourage: Encourage Janie to establish good study habits. Encourage the rest of the class to maintain good study habits when Janie tries to disrupt them.

6. Tommy Pet much prefers to linger near the teacher's desk than to interact with his fellow students. Whenever he is invited by other students to participate in group projects, his standard response is, "Nah, I can't. I have to help Ms. Jones."

   Behaviors to discourage: _____

   _____

   _____

   Behaviors to encourage: _____

   _____

   _____

- - - - - - - - - - - - - - - - - -

   Behaviors to discourage: Discourage Tommy from lingering near the teacher's desk. Discourage Tommy from making his standard negative response when he is approached by other students.

   Behavior to encourage: Encourage Tommy to enter into activities away from the teacher's desk. Encourage Tommy to say yes when urged to participate in social projects. Encourage other students to invite Tommy's participation.

Thus far we have considered the types of situations and behaviors which might serve as targets for the application of Operant Learning Theory. Next we need to devise the actual procedures one would apply to a particular problem. First, however, we must consider the basic principles underlying applied Operant Learning Theory.

PRINCIPLES OF APPLIED OPERANT LEARNING THEORY

Applied Operant Learning Theory is based upon three principles:

1. Behaviors followed by reinforcing events increase in frequency.
2. Behaviors not followed by reinforcement decrease in frequency.
3. Behaviors followed by punishment decrease in frequency.

Let's discuss these principles one by one. The first principle in applied Operant Learning Theory is that behaviors followed by reinforcing events increase in frequency. An understanding of the concept of a reinforcer is important. Technically defined, a reinforcer is any consequence (event, tangible reward, praise, or the like) which follows a behavior and results in an increase in frequency of that behavior. The concept of a reinforcer is rather subtle. A given event or thing which is a reinforcer for some people may not be a reinforcer for others. Let's take money as an example. Most of us work because we get paid to do so. And, in general, most of us would work harder (increase the frequency of our work) in high-paying jobs than we would in low-paying jobs. However, for many people money does not serve as a reinforcer. Such people frequently seek and stay in jobs that they find interesting rather than choosing jobs on the basis of the rate of pay. Others are compulsive workers (sometimes dubbed "workaholics") who would work hard at any job.

The fact that particular events or objects serve as reinforcers for some, but not for others, is very important in applying Operant Learning Theory to educational problems. A teacher might find that most students are responsive to verbal praise and recognition. That is, behaviors which are praised or recognized will be likely to occur again. However, some students are not responsive to verbal praise or recognition. For these students a teacher must find some other means of encouraging positive behaviors—that is, some other event or object which serves as a reinforcer.

At this point you may be asking, "If an event or object is a reinforcer for some people, but not for others, how will I recognize a reinforcer?" You must observe behavior. If an event or object causes an increase in frequency of behavior when it follows that behavior, you probably have discovered a reinforcer. If an increase in frequency of behavior doesn't occur, you know the event or object is not a reinforcer. The fact that behavior increases in frequency when it is followed by a reinforcing event suggests how this principle is used in applying Operant Learning Theory to an educational problem: The event reinforces students for performing positive behaviors. If, for example, a teacher wants to encourage good study habits, he or she must reinforce behaviors such as sitting quietly at a desk, working on problems, reading and note taking.

This first principle also implies that reinforcers can increase the frequency of _inappropriate_ behaviors. So, for example, the "class clown" frequently performs to attract attention and recognition from the teacher or from a peer group. In this case, attention and recognition serve as reinforcers for behavior the teacher considers to be inappropriate.

The list below will give you an idea of the variety of events which have proven to be successful reinforcers for encouraging appropriate behaviors in educational institutions:

Social reinforcers such as praise or physical affection

Tangible rewards such as candy, toys, or other desirable items

Token rewards, such as chips, that can be accumulated and traded in for tangible rewards.

Access to high-frequency activities (activities a child does often). The child may be allowed more time on a favorite subject, extra recess time, a visit with friends, or assignment to a preferred classroom role such as safety patrol, blackboard monitor, the like. The idea that access to high-frequency activities can serve as a reinforcer to increase low-frequency activities (activities a child does not do often) is known as Premack's Principle.

---

7. To gain some practice in identifying reinforcers, perform the following exercise. First, list four things you do frequently. After making this list, try to identify a reinforcer which encourages you to engage in these frequent behaviors.

Frequent Behaviors	Reinforcers
1. _____	_____
2. _____	_____
3. _____	_____
4. _____	_____

- - - - - - - - - - - - - - - - - -

Obviously, no one answer is correct. However, you might be interested in a list prepared by one of the authors of this book:

1. Teaching	Societal recognition; salary; pleasure at seeing students advance in knowledge
2. Writing articles and books	Professional status and recognition; money (sometimes)
3. Reading for pleasure	Relaxation and relief from tension; broader scope of knowledge

4.   Playing tennis   Physical relaxation; satisfaction
                                        of competitive urge; pleasure at
                                        growth of physical skill

The second principle in applied Operant Learning Theory is that behaviors not followed by reinforcement decrease in frequency. This principle is based on the assumption that humans (as well as other animals) are reinforcement-seeking organisms. If a particular behavior leads to reinforcement, the behavior will probably be repeated (as stated in our first principle). If a particular behavior does not lead to reinforcement, it is less likely to be repeated. This second generality is called the principle of extinction. From the teacher's point of view, the idea is to identify and cut off the reinforcers which are encouraging inappropriate student behaviors. If, for example, students are misbehaving to attract the teacher's attention or the attention of peers, the misbehavior will decrease in frequency if attention is no longer given to the misbehavior.

Mr. Johnson has been having a very difficult time with Charley Brown. Every time Mr. Johnson asks his class a question, Charley begins to jump up and down and shout, "I know! I know! Call on me!" Mr. Johnson's standard response has been to stop everything and remind Charley that everyone knows he is a bright boy but that he really should give the other students an opportunity to answer questions. Charley just nods his head, smiles, and does exactly the same thing the next time a question is asked.

8.   What is likely to be the reinforcer which is maintaining Charley's shouting out behavior? _____

_____

_____

— — — — — — — — — — — — — — — — — — — —

Mr. Johnson's response is probably serving as a reinforcer for Charley's behavior. It focuses the attention of the entire class on Charley while he is told how bright he is. Rather than putting a stop to Charley's behavior, as Mr. Johnson had intended, his response is encouraging the behavior.

9.   What strategy might Mr. Johnson use to eliminate Charley's problem behavior? _____

_____

_____

— — — — — — — — — — — — — — — — — — — —

Charley's shouting-out behavior might be reduced simply by ignoring it. If the behavior is no longer reinforced, it will decline in frequency. You may even have mentioned that Mr. Johnson should try to increase the frequency of positive behavior (by reinforcing hand-raising) as well as decrease the frequency of inappropriate behavior.

The third principle in applied Operant Learning Theory is that <u>behaviors followed by punishment decrease in frequency.</u> The concept of a punishing event is the mirror image of the concept of a reinforcing event. We know that an event is reinforcing if, and only if, behavior either increases in frequency or is maintained after that event. Conversely, we know an event is punishing if, and only if, the behavior following that event declines in frequency. This concept is very important, because teachers frequently deliver what they believe to be punishment (verbal reprimands, sending students into the hall, or the like) only to find that, if anything, the behaviors they are trying to punish <u>increase</u> in frequency.

Later we will discuss two different kinds of punishment. They are:

<u>Physical or psychological punishment,</u> such as scolding or a rap on the knuckles.

<u>Removal from a reinforcing environment,</u> such as taking a child from the classroom and sending him or her to another room away from peers. Notice that this form of punishment involves the assumption that the classroom is a place where students have access to a variety of reinforcers (teacher attention, peer attention, play and study materials, and so on). If the classroom is not a source of reinforcement to the child, the this form of punishment is futile. However, very few children would rather be in isolation than in the classroom. If you have such children in your classroom, you should probably seek outside help for them.

10. Ms. Hugalot is a very affectionate teacher who simply loves "all of my little children. " One boy in her class, Tommy Spike, worries Ms. Hugalot a great deal, because he seems rather shy in the classroom. Ms. Hugalot has employed her own special style to draw Tommy out. Whenever Tommy answers a question correctly or does a good job on his homework, Ms. Hugalot makes sure she is in position to give Tommy a "big hug and a kiss. " Lately, Tommy seems to be answering questions less often and the quality of his homework has slipped. What might be wrong?

_____

_____

_____

_____

_____

It's likely Tommy doesn't view the "big hug and kiss" as reinforcing. In fact, his behavior suggests that the teacher's affection is serving as a punishment. As you are probably aware, preadolescent boys often view displays of affection from females as sources of embarrassment.

REVIEW

11. What two characteristics should be present in a situation where Operant Learning Theory might be appropriately applied?

_____

_____

_____

_____

_____

- - - - - - - - - - - - - - - - - -

    1. Normal procedures for dealing with students do not work.
    2. The problem in question involves an observable student behavior.

12. Upon what three principles is applied Operant Learning Theory based?

_____

_____

_____

_____

- - - - - - - - - - - - - - - - - -

    1. Behaviors followed by reinforcing events increase in frequency.
    2. Behaviors not followed by reinforcement decrease in frequency.
    3. Behaviors followed by punishment decrease in frequency.

ISSUES IN THE USE OF OPERANT LEARNING THEORY

Before we discuss ways to apply Operant Learning Theory (frequently called behavior modification), we should discuss some of the issues which are often raised with regard to the theory's application. The intent of the classroom application of Operant Learning Theory is to modify student behavior. Modification is attained through the systematic use of rewards and punishment. The intent to modify or control human behavior has been, and continues to be, a source of controversy. We wish to state our perspective toward these controversial issues, emphasizing the personal nature of this perspective. Many people would take a different position on the desirability of using Operant Learning principles. Our purpose is to expose you to these issues in the hope that each of you will be able to make an informed decision about whether applied Operant Learning Theory has a place in the classroom.

One issue frequently raised with regard to the use of Operant Learning Theory is teacher use of reward and punishment to modify or control student behavior. Discussion of this issue actually raises two separate questions. The first is whether or not teachers should use reward and punishment at all. Most of you will recognize that this practice is little in question. Teachers always have used, and probably always will use, reward and punishment in their classrooms. The second question is the real crux of the matter: Should teachers use reward and punishment in a systematic fashion to control student behavior? On the one hand, many have argued that Operant Learning Theory places a tool in the hands of a teacher which, because of ignorance or even malevolence, can be used for nonbeneficial purposes. Others have argued that the judicious application of Operant Learning Theory has great promise as a means for attaining beneficial academic and social goals. Our own view is that the potential for good far outweighs the potential for harm. Operant Learning Theory can be applied to a variety of important educational problems, and we would hope that those responsible for overseeing our educational institutions (school boards, administrators, fellow teachers) would halt the misapplication of the theory.

A related issue is the restriction of freedom of an individual student who is subjected to Operant Learning practices. Each of you should think about this very complex philosophical issue; we would not pretend to resolve the issue for you. However, several observations may be relevant. First, the very nature of child-rearing, and even of our society itself, involves placing reasonable limits on individual freedom. Freedom, as we define it, is the opportunity to select from a variety of available choices. Thus, a person who has a wide variety of options from which to choose has more freedom than the person who chooses from a very restricted range of options.

Let's apply that definition to a concrete situation. Let's say that you were solely responsible for the education of a boy named Bill, and another teacher was solely responsible for the education of a similarly capable boy named John. Further, let's say that Bill wasn't terribly interested in academic subjects and that you took the position that when Bill became interested in learning something, he would come to you, and you would teach him. Let's say that the other teacher took a very different view. He was convinced that John should be competent in the traditional academic areas; though initially John was no more interested than Bill, the teacher used responsible Operant Learning procedures to achieve his ends. Years pass, and both boys are now ready to be graduated from high school. Bill is woefully weak in basic academic skills, whereas John has progressed well and can compete academically with virtually any other high school graduate. We suggest that John, at that point, has many more options about what he does with his life than Bill. And, further, we suggest that John is a freer man because he possesses this wider range of options.

A final issue we wish to consider deals with what is called "love of learning for learning's own sake." Many critics of applied Operant Learning Theory have argued that students who are systematically rewarded for learning will come to expect a reward, and when the time comes, as it must, when the reward is no longer given, they will show little interest in further learning. This argument has merit, and the danger involved necessitates considerable care in using Operant Learning techniques. For example, we would recommend that Operant Learning Theory be applied only in situations where other approaches do not work. Further, we would recommend that steps be taken to withdraw use of the techniques as rapidly as possible, through methods we will introduce later in this chapter.

One further point in the "love of learning" criticism deserves discussion. Surely the goal of all educators, practitioners of Operant Learning Theory included, is that their students come to love learning for the sake of learning. But how does one instill love of learning? While humans are innately curious, they have no innate love for algebra, history, or a Tolstoy novel. Students must acquire an enormous number of prerequisite skills before these subjects become meaningful to them. The use of Operant Learning Theory will not provide a student with an appreciation of the genius of Shakespeare or the lucid elegance of relativity theory, but the theory can be used as a useful tool to insure that students who might otherwise not do so acquire the skills that may someday allow them to come to love these various academic pursuits.

APPLIED OPERANT LEARNING THEORY IN PRACTICE

In this section, we will first discuss three different procedures for applying Operant Learning Theory to an educational problem. We wil then present the steps for designing a program based on applied Operant Learning Theory. This discussion will prepare you actually to apply the theory to sample situations in the next chapter.

The three main approaches to applying Operant Learning Theory, in order of preference, are:

1. Social reinforcement of appropriate behavior and extinction of inappropriate behavior.
2. Token reinforcement of appropriate behavior.
3. Punishment of inappropriate behavior and reinforcement of appropriate behavior.

The idea behind the first approach—social reinforcement of appropriate behavior and extinction of inappropriate behavior—is that the teacher is a potent source of social reinforcement. Teacher recognition in the form of praise, a pat on the back, or even a smile is an effective reinforcer for most younger children. The teacher can use such recognition to encourage positive behaviors. At the same time that positive behaviors are being encouraged (through teacher social reinforcement), negative or inappropriate behaviors can be discouraged by withholding social reinforcement for inappropriate behaviors. As an example, let's say you want to encourage a particular child to stay in her seat rather than wandering aimlessly around the classroom. Using this approach, one strategy would be to reinforce the child socially when she is in her seat and ignore the child (withhold social reinforcement) when she is out of her seat. Withholding reinforcement is part of the process we call extinction.

This approach works particularly well under certain conditions. First, students must be responsive to teacher-delivered social reinforcement. If students value the praise or recognition of the teacher, the technique will work. Generally speaking, younger children value teacher praise and recognition. However, older children are frequently less responsive to teacher-delivered social reinforcement, or may be totally unresponsive to it. Adolescents, in particular, are often much more responsive to social reinforcement delivered by peer groups than to social reinforcement delivered by teachers. Where students are not responsible to teacher-delivered social reinforcement, one of the other approaches, to be discussed later, is called for.

For social reinforcement to work well, the target behaviors (those behaviors which are reinforced or ignored) must also be easily defined and easy to observe. Consider the following case, for example. Mr. Brown wants to improve Johnny Jones' work habits. Johnny brings Mr. Brown a completed homework assignment which has been done very well. Mr. Brown praises Johnny for his "very good work." As it happens, Johnny has copied the homework assignment from a friend. Thus Johnny has just been reinforced for cheating, not for his good work habits. What Mr. Brown should have done is to select for reinforcement specific target behaviors, such as reading quietly, working on problems, or writing. The assumption is that if the frequency of these specific observable behaviors increases, the overall quality of Johnny's work will improve. If reinforcement is not provided for these specific behaviors but is provided instead for much more global behavioral indicators, some inappropriate kinds of behavior may be reinforced. We are not suggesting that "good work" should not be reinforced. Rather, if the goal is to improve work habits, then specific behavioral indicators of good work habits should be identified for systematic reinforcement.

Under certain other conditions, however, the social-reinforcement approach is unlikely to be effective. The first we have already mentioned; if students are unresponsive to teacher-delivered social reinforcement, the approach will not work. Second, if the rate of inappropriate behavior is so high that little appropriate behavior remains to be reinforced, social reinforcement probably won't work. Third, if the student's inappropriate behavior is so intense that it endangers the student or other people, the use of this approach is prevented. If this last condition is present, the teacher simply cannot afford to ignore the inappropriate behavior. An example of this sort of behavior is the throwing of heavy objects.

Under any of these conditions, the social reinforcement approach is not recommended. Teachers faced with these conditions should consider one or the other of the two approaches we will discuss next.

Early in the school year, Harriet Simpson (a second grader) began to throw mild tantrums in Ms. Gadin's class. Ms. Gadin, feeling unequipped to handle such behaviors, began to send Harriet to the principal's office every time a tantrum occurred. To her dismay, sending Harriet to the principal's office seemed to have little effect. In fact, the rate of Harriet's tantrums seemed to be increasing. Based on what you have learned in the previous section, answer the following questions about this situation.

13. Are the conditions present which would justify the use of the social-reinforcement approach? Why, or why not?

_____

_____

_____

- - - - - - - - - - - - - - - - - -

Yes, the conditions are present which would justify trying this approach. First, as a second grader, Harriet is likely to be responsive to adult social reinforcement. This assumption is supported by the fact that going to see the principal seems to act as a reinforcer. Second, the tantrums which are the principal cause of the problem are easily observable, as are the alternative types of positive behavior (sitting quietly, positive social interactions, and so on). Also, the problem behavior has persisted for quite a while, and other methods have been tried.

14. Are any conditions present which would negate the usefulness of the social-reinforcement approach? If so, identify them.

_____

_____

_____

- - - - - - - - - - - - - - - - - -

Probably not. Evidence suggests that Harriet is responsive to adult social reinforcement. In addition, the inappropriate behavior is not so frequent or so intense that other procedures would be called for.

15. If this approach were used, identify several behaviors which Ms. Gadin should socially reinforce.

_____

_____

_____

- - - - - - - - - - - - - - - - - -

_____

Many possibilities exist, such as sitting quietly, positive social behaviors with peers and Ms. Gadin, reading, and doing art work.

16. If this approach were used, identify the behavior which Ms. Gadin should extinguish (withhold social reinforcement for).

_____

_____

_____

- - - - - - - - - - - - - - - - - -

The tantrum behavior.

The second approach, token reinforcement of appropriate behavior, involves giving some sort of token that can be turned in later for a tangible reward (for example, candy, toys, recess time, outings, or tickets to events). Token reinforcement is thought to be stronger than social reinforcement and to be effective in situations where social reinforcement has little impact. The tokens can be poker chips, stars, checkmarks on paper, or any other item that can be accumulated, and later exchanged for a tangible reward.

In this approach, tokens, rather than actual tangible rewards, are used because they allow more flexibility in administering the reinforcement. For example, tokens can be delivered immediately following the occurrence of a desirable behavior, whereas immediate delivery of a tangible reward might be cumbersome or impossible. Also, when tokens are used, the teacher can control the "exchange rate"—the number of tokens required for a particular tangible reward. If tangible rewards alone are used, such control is impossible.

Three general guidelines should be followed when using a token-reinforcement approach. The first is that tokens should be given immediately following the occurrence of the desired behavior. For example, if the desired behavior involves study habits, the tokens should be given immediately after the occurrence of the desired study behavior. Delaying the giving of tokens until the end of the day, for example, generally results in the failure of the token-reinforcement approach. The second guideline is that tokens should be phased out as soon as possible. Generally this phasing out is done in the following manner: When the program first starts, the token schedule is fairly "rich"—that is, tokens are given frequently and in sufficient quantity to encourage the students to perform the targeted behaviors. As the program goes on, and as the frequency of the target behaviors increases, the schedule becomes "leaner." Tokens are given less frequently and in smaller quantity, until a point is reached where the tokens are phased out entirely. The intent of this technique is to reinforce liberally in the initial phases of the program in order to establish the desired behaviors. Once the behaviors are established, naturally occurring reinforcers, such as peer approval and improved capability, can be gradually substituted to maintain the desired behaviors.

The mention of naturally occurring reinforcers brings us to our third guideline. <u>Administration of tokens should be combined with social reinforcement.</u> If tokens are paired with social reinforcement, previously ineffective social reinforcement will begin to take on reinforcing value. The phasing out of tokens and the substitution of another form of reinforcement are done so that students do not develop a permanent expectation of a tangible "payoff" for performing certain kinds of behavior. In addition to social reinforcement by teachers, other forms of reinforcement frequently come into play in maintaining newly established positive behaviors. For example, if the token-reinforcement system results in an increase in frequency of appropriate social behaviors, and the more appropriate social behaviors result in more intimate social relations with peers, then the social relations themselves serve as reinforcers for maintaining the appropriate social behaviors. Likewise, such reinforcing events as approval for better grades on report cards can serve to maintain improved study habits.

Token-reinforcement approaches are particularly useful in situations where students are not normally responsive to teacher social reinforcement. For example, token-reinforcement approaches have been shown to work particularly with adolescents, a group which is sometimes very unresponsive to teacher recognition. If you decide to use a token-reinforcement approach, you should take particular care to assure that students do not develop the expectation that appropriate behavior always deserves a direct payoff. The gradual phasing out of the token system and the gradual substitution of other forms of reinforcement should help you accomplish this purpose, as we shall discuss.

17. The following exercise will give you some practice in developing the initial step in a token-reinforcement system (more practice will be provided in the next chapter). Imagine you are a teacher in a junior high school, and you want to initiate a token-reinforcement system. Your first step is to develop a "menu" of tangible items or events which would be desirable to junior high school students. Tokens obtained for desirable behavior could then be traded in for items or events from this menu. List items which you would consider appropriate for inclusion on the menu.

_____

_____

_____

- - - - - - - - - - - - - - - - - -

Your list might include items such as:

   Independent work
   Permission to play ball during lunch
   Free choice of a book to read
   A special privilege during a study hall
   Permission to work on a project with a special friend

Permission to help other students in an area of personal expertise
Permission to visit with a special friend

Many other possibilities are available. Your list may be quite different.
The point is simply to identify activities your students like best.

The third approach is the punishment of inappropriate behavior and reinforcement of appropriate behavior. The concept of punishment is quite familiar
to most people. However, when the term "punishment" is used in the context
of applied Operant Learning Theory, it has a specialized meaning. In applied
Operant Learning Theory, an event is considered punishment if it produces a
decrease in frequency of the behavior which precedes it. In accord with this
definition, two kinds of punishment have been used in applied Operant Learning programs. The first involves the delivery of a noxious stimulus. This
meaning of punishment is a common one and involves the delivery of an event
which the student finds physically or psychologically unpleasant. Spanking and
verbal reprimands are examples of this type of punishment. The second kind
of punishment involves removing the student from a reinforcing environment.
This sort of event, even though we would not commonly think of it as punishment, produces the same kinds of results as the delivery of a noxious stimulus. For example, a student who "acts out" to gain the recognition of his or
her peers can be sent to a "time out" room, contingent upon poor behavior. In
a "time out" situation, the student is denied access to sources of reinforcement (peer recognition), and the rate of acting out should decrease.

Punishment should be used by teachers only as a last resort, since several
deleterious side effects may occur when punishment is used. For example,
students may learn to cheat, play hookey, feign sickness, or become very
passive in order to avoid the delivery of punishment. Therefore, punishment
should be used only in extreme situations.

Two kinds of situations might call for punishment. The first is when inappropriate behavior is so frequent that no appropriate behavior remains to be
reinforced. In this situation, the two previous approaches—social reinforcement or token reinforcement—would not work because the student rarely performs positive behaviors which deserve reinforcement. In this situation the
rate of inappropriate behavior must be brought down in order to allow the
appearance of positive behaviors.

The second situation where punishment might be called for is when the
inappropriate behavior is so intense that it endangers the student or other
people. Actions such as throwing heavy objects or hitting other students or
unsafe "daredevil" activities must be suppressed immediately. The teacher
cannot afford to ignore such behaviors, and punishment can be used to suppress them.

Given a situation that calls for punishment, the teacher should, if at all
possible, choose to punish by removing the student from a reinforcing environment rather than by delivering a noxious stimulus. Removal from a reinforcing environment procedure is much less likely to produce deleterious side
effects than is the delivery of a noxious stimulus. The teacher should strive to

maintain the classroom as a source of reinforcement, not punishment, for the student. If punishment involves delivery of a noxious stimulus in the classroom, the student may come to view the classroom, and perhaps school in general, as a punishing environment. The student who holds such a view may develop all sorts of behaviors in order to avoid or escape this punishing environment. On the other hand, if the teacher can maintain the classroom as a reinforcing environment, and make use of removal from that environment following inappropriate behaviors, the student may modify his or her behaviors in order to avoid removal from that environment.

The use of punishment following inappropriate behaviors represents only half of this approach. The remaining half involves the reinforcement of appropriate behaviors, which may involve the use of social reinforcement or, if that is unsuitable, token reinforcement. The intent of this approach is to suppress (through punishment) inappropriate behavior which is so frequent or so severe that use of other approaches is not possible. As the behaviors justifying the use of punishment begin to disappear, the punishment approach should evolve into either one of the two positive-reinforcement approaches.

Robert Einstein is the budding boy genius of Ms. Rand's chemistry class. One day Robert decides that it would be great fun to drop a chunk of pure sodium into a sink full of water. The result of this action is that considerable heat is generated, along with hydrogen gas, which is highly explosive. Robert drops the sodium and is highly amused by the sputtering and spattering produced in the sink. Ms. Rand, however, is not amused.

18. Are the conditions present in this situation which would justify the use of punishment? If so, what are they?

_____

_____

_____

- - - - - - - - - - - - - - - - - - -

Indeed they are. Robert's behavior clearly endangers himself and the other students in the class (his action falls into the category of intensely inappropriate behavior). Ms. Rand would be derelict in her responsibilities as a teacher if she did not take steps to suppress the behavior.

19. Assuming that the decision is to punish Robert, how should he be punished?

_____

_____

_____

- - - - - - - - - - - - - - - - -

The teacher may respond in two ways. First, common sense dictates that Robert and the rest of the class should be given a lecture about safety practices in a chemistry lab. Second, Robert should be prevented from attending chemistry class for at least one period. Assuming Robert enjoys the class, this punishment may be sufficient to suppress any further occurrences of the behavior.

These three approaches commonly used when applying Operant Learning Theory to educational problems are not listed in random order but, rather in a preferred order of use. In all cases, the teacher should strive for a social-reinforcement program; that is, the teacher should first consider whether or not a social-reinforcement program would be effective. If the student will not respond to social reinforcement delivered by the teacher, and the teacher knows this, then a token economy should next be considered. If the inappropriate behavior is so frequent that virtually no positive behavior remains to be reinforced or the behavior is so severe that the student or others might be endangered by it, then a program of punishment combined with reinforcement might be necessary. Even if a teacher institutes a program of punishment combined with reinforcement, the desirable approach is to work up to a social-reinforcement program as soon as possible.

We have considered the type of situation in which Operant Learning Theory might be applied. We have also discussed the basic principles underlying applied Operant Learning Theory and three useful approaches to solving educational problems. We will now introduce the steps involved in implementing an applied Operant Learning Theory program.

REVIEW

20. What are the three Operant Learning Theory approaches discussed earlier in the chapter?

_____

_____

_____

- - - - - - - - - - - - - - - -

1. Social reinforcement of appropriate behavior and extinction of inappropriate behavior.
2. Token reinforcement of appropriate behavior.
3. Punishment of inappropriate behavior and reinforcement of appropriate behavior.

STEPS IN IMPLEMENTING
AN APPLIED OPERANT LEARNING THEORY PROGRAM

Teachers who are interested in developing an applied Operant Learning Theory approach to an educational problem should follow these steps:

1. State the goal of the program (in behavioral terms).
2. Select the target behaviors for modification.
3. Choose the appropriate Operant Learning Theory approach.
4. Explain the rules to the students.
5. Systematically apply the rules.

We will now discuss each of these steps in turn.

State the goal of the program in behavioral terms. The goal of the program is a statement of the desired behavior upon completion of the program. This statement should include two elements: the desired level of inappropriate behavior and the desired level of appropriate behavior. Remember, the intent of the program should be to replace undesirable behavior with more positive forms of behavior. For example, shouting-out answers should be replaced with hand-raising and answering when called upon.

Select the target behaviors for modification. This second step involves the selection of specific target behaviors which are indicators of the broader goals formulated in the first step. For example, let's say that the goals of a program are to reduce the level of inappropriate social activity to approximately 10 percent of measured intervals (we will discuss this measurement in the next chapter) and to increase the incidence of appropriate study behaviors to approximately 90 percent of measured intervals. Application of this step would then involve identifying specific indicators of both inappropriate behaviors (for example, being out of the seat, talking with neighbors, writing notes to friends) and appropriate behaviors (for example, reading quietly, writing papers, working problems.)

Choose the appropriate applied Operant Learning Theory approach to use. The teacher should always strive for a social-reinforcement program. However, if the students will not respond to reinforcement controlled by a teacher, a token-reinforcement program might be necessary. If the inappropriate behavior by the student is too violent or extreme, it might be necessary to go to a punishment followed by reward program. No matter which approach is decided upon, the teacher should strive for social reinforcement. This means phasing out token economies and gradually substituting social reinforcement or, if punishment followed by reward is chosen, phasing out the punishment for a token reinforcement or social-reinforcement program.

Explain the rules to the students. This fourth step is simply good common sense. All teachers should make their rules for classroom behavior very explicit, by means of verbal explanation to the children and the making of occasional reference to them. The rules may even be posted on the wall in the classroom. The teacher can then reward concurrence with the rules or can punish or ignore transgressions. Sometimes the target behavior for the

Operant Learning program is not explicitly stated in the general classroom rules. For example, no teacher is likely to formulate a rule prohibiting sneezing in his or her classroom (but remember Billy Smith?). When a behavior not covered by the rules becomes a problem, the teacher should individually explain to the child in question that the particular behavior is offensive and indicate the consequences of continuing the behavior. Thus, a teacher should follow three practices regarding rules for both an entire classroom and an individual student.

1. Make rules for behavior explicit.
2. Make the consequences of not following the rules explicit. For example, "Billy, the first time you sneeze during the day I am doing to give you a warning. The second time you will lose your recess privileges."
3. Reward behavior that is consistent with the rules and consistently apply the consequences of inappropriate behavior. The teacher who tells a child that a particular consequence will follow the occurrence of an inappropriate behavior, and then ignores the behavior when it occurs, is virtually guaranteed to have trouble.

Systematically apply the rules. This fifth step involves providing reinforcement for appropriate target behaviors and either ignoring or punishing inappropriate behaviors. Inappropriate behaviors should be specified in the classroom rules or discussed personally with individual students. In applying rules, you must follow one critical rule: be consistent! Haphazard or sporadic enforcement of the rules makes matters worse, not better.

ADDITIONAL READINGS ON OPERANT LEARNING THEORY

Carpenter, F. The Skinner Primer: Beyond Freedom and Dignity. New York: The Free Press, 1974.

Hill, W. F. Learning: A Survey of Psychological Interpretations. San Francisco: Chandler Publishing Co., 1963.

Holland, J. G., and Skinner, B. F. The Analysis of Behavior. New York: McGraw-Hill, 1961.

Keller, F. S. Learning: Reinforcement Theory (2nd ed.). New York: Random House, 1969.

Reynolds, G. S. A Primer of Operant Conditioning. Glenville, Illinois: Scott, Foresman and Company, 1968.

Sahakian, W. S. Psychology of Learning: Systems, Models, and Theories. Chicago: Markham Publishing Co., 1970.

Skinner, B. F. Science and Human Behavior. New York: Macmillan Company, 1953.

SELF-TEST

This self-test is designed to show you whether or not you have mastered the objectives of Chapter 1. Answer each question to the best of your ability, based on what you have learned in this chapter. Correct answers are given following the test.

1. A teacher should consider applying Operant Learning Theory to a situation having what two general characteristics?

    _____

    _____

    _____

2. List the three principles upon which Operant Learning Theory is based.

    a. _____

       _____

    b. _____

       _____

    c. _____

       _____

3. Write "Social reinforcement," "Token economy" or "Punishment/Reward" next to each described situation, indicating the approach you feel ought to be implemented.

Approach	Situation
_____	a. Although all of her students highly respect Ms. Smith one of the boys in her class occasionally shouts at other students and disrupts the class.
_____	b. Mr. McIntyre simply cannot get a number of his students to do their homework, though he has the entire class trying to put pressure on these "backsliders."
_____	c. Billy is causing great concern; he has a penchant for throwing school materials about and is apt to hurt someone.

<u>Approach</u>   <u>Situation</u>

_____ d. Ms. Gomey is working with an unruly
                             group of second graders who will not
                             respond to her with respect, affec-
                             tion, or fear. She must bring them
                             under control if any learning is to
                             take place.

_____ e. Sally is a whirling dervish. She will
                             not stop talking or slow down long
                             enough to pay attention and is a total
                             disruption to the class. The teacher
                             can find no positive behaviors of
                             Sally's to reinforce!

_____ f. Adrienne and Paulette are good stu-
                             dents, but their homework assign-
                             ments and test scores have started
                             to fall off. Ms. Johnson feels that,
                             with only a little effort, she can get
                             them back on the right track.

ANSWERS TO SELF-TEST

Compare your answers to the questions on the self-test with the answers given below. If all of your answers are correct, you are ready to go on to the next chapter. If you missed any questions, review the appropriate parts of the chapter before you go on.

1. A teacher should consider applying Operant Learning Theory when normal procedures for dealing with students do not work and where the problem in question involves observable student behaviors.

2. The three principles of Operant Learning Theory are:

    a. Behaviors followed by reinforcing events increase in frequency.
    b. Behaviors not followed by reinforcement decrease in frequency.
    c. Behaviors followed by punishment decrease in frequency.

3. a. Social reinforcement
    b. Token economy
    c. Punishment/reward
    d. Token economy
    e. Punishment/reward
    f. Social reinforcement

CHAPTER TWO
Application of Operant Learning Theory to Educational Problems

Chapter 1 was concerned with the basics of applied Operant Learning Theory. Having gained some familiarity with the basics, we are now ready to practice actual applications of the theory. When presented with a situation which calls for the use of applied Operant Learning Theory, you will be able to:

1. Select inappropriate behaviors which should be reduced in frequency.
2. Select appropriate behaviors which should be increased in frequency.
3. Develop a list of classroom rules.
4. Collect and use data for the purposes of setting and evaluating program goals.
5. Develop and implement a reinforcement schedule.
6. Properly use data-recording techniques.

IDENTIFYING GOALS AND TARGET BEHAVIORS

Since the purpose of this chapter is to provide practice in applying Operant Learning Theory, let's begin by looking at a situation suitable for application of the theory.

Imagine that you are a fifth grade teacher in a suburban school system. One of the students in your class, Herman Bonham, has driven you to your wits' end. Herman is large for his age, and he is the classroom bully. He frequently hits, pushes, or annoys the other students in the class. He seems to be out of his seat most of the time and is continually doing things that disrupt the class and interfere with his own learning and the learning of other students. It is apparent that he never studies, since his homework assignments are rarely turned in, and when he does turn them in they are done very poorly. You have tried everything you can think of with Herman; you have lectured, cajoled, threatened, and even pleaded with him, but nothing seems to work. Herman remains the terror of your classroom. As a last resort, before having Herman removed from your classroom, you decide to try applied Operant Learning Theory to improve Herman's behavior.

1. Based on what you learned in Chapter 1, what is the first step you would take in implementing an applied Operant Learning Theory program?

    _____

    _____

    _____

- - - - - - - - - - - - - - - - - - - -

    You should state precisely the goals of the applied Operant Learning Program.

2. Based on the above description, write a set of behaviorally defined goals for Herman.

    _____

    _____

    _____

    _____

    _____

    _____

- - - - - - - - - - - - - - - - - - - -

    Your set of goals should be similar to the following:

    The program should decrease the frequency of:

    Herman's aggressive and abusive behaviors towards other students
    Herman's out-of-seat behaviors
    Herman's behaviors which disrupt the entire class

    The program should increase the frequency of:

    Positive social behaviors towards other students
    Sitting in seat at appropriate times
    Handing in homework assignments
    High-quality school work

3. After you have developed a set of general objectives for Herman, what is the next step in implementing an applied Operant Learning Theory program?

    _____

    _____

- - - - - - - - - - - - - - - -

Select specific behaviors which will be targets for the Operant Learning Theory procedures.

4. Based on the information you have about Herman and your own experiences with students like him, prepare a list of specific behaviors which should <u>decrease</u> <u>in</u> <u>frequency</u> (inappropriate behaviors) when the program is applied. (NOTE: This list should include specific behaviors to eliminate. The list should be longer and much more specific than the goals statements you produced.)

_____

_____

_____

_____

_____

- - - - - - - - - - - - - - - - -

Your list should be similar to the following list of specific behaviors which should decrease in frequency:

Grabbing objects	Whistling loudly
Kicking	Being out of seat without
Hitting with objects	permission
Throwing objects	Running
Biting	Jumping
Spitting at other students	Moving chairs around room
Yelling out comments	Banging books
Yelling at other students	Tapping pencil
Coughing loudly	Hitting hands against desk
Making obscene noises	

Before we go on, we must consider some practical problems. The answer above listed eighteen specific behaviors. Later in this chapter we will discuss how to write classroom rules and how to set up procedures for recording the frequency of occurrence of each of these specified target behaviors. These activities will be simplified if we group target behaviors into several categories. This categorization will allow you to write rules concerned with general categories of behavior; the specific behaviors can then serve as examples for the general category. In addition, dividing a large list of behaviors into several categories will expedite the data-recording process. For example, it is much easier to record quickly the occurrence of a given behavior if you know that the behavior belongs in a given category. You need only move to the category and find the specific behavior within that category. In contrast, if your list of behaviors is not divided into categories, you must make a longer search through the list to find a specific behavior and record its occurrence.

With the above considerations in mind, let's look again at the list of Herman's behaviors.

5. Divide the list of behaviors below into several categories. You should group together behaviors which have something in common. When you have divided the list into categories, devise a label which describes each general category. (We divided our list into four categories.)

Category Label	Behavior
	Grabbing objects
	Kicking
	Hitting with objects
	Throwing objects
	Biting
	Spitting at other students
	Yelling out comments
	Yelling at other students
	Coughing loudly
	Making obscene noises
	Whistling loudly
	Being out of seat without permission
	Running
	Jumping
	Moving chairs around room
	Banging books
	Tapping pencil
	Hitting hands against desk

- - - - - - - - - - - - - - - - - - - -

Our labels and category groupings are presented below.

Category Label	Behavior
Annoying and aggressive behavior with other students	Grabbing objects
	Kicking
	Hitting with objects
	Throwing objects
	Biting
	Spitting at other students
Vocal disruptions of class	Yelling out comments
	Yelling at other students
	Coughing loudly

Category Label	Behavior
Physical activities	Making obscene noises
	Whistling loudly
	Being out of seat without permission
	Running
	Jumping
	Moving chairs around room
Disruptive noises with objects	Banging books
	Tapping pencil
	Hitting hands against desk

Your groups and labels are probably different from ours. However, for illustrative purposes, we will use the four categories identified above.

We now have specified the inappropriate behaviors which will be targets for an applied Operant Learning Theory approach, and we have categorized those behaviors to simplify rule writing and data recording. The next task is to specify positive behaviors which will also be targets for the applied Operant Learning Theory approach.

Earlier in the chapter we suggested that some goals of our applied Operant Learning Theory approach should be to increase the frequency of:

Positive social behaviors towards other students
Sitting in seat at appropriate times
Handing in homework assignments
High-quality school work

---

6. Given those goals, prepare a list of specific behaviors which should increase in frequency for each of the four goals. That is, what behaviors by Herman would indicate to you that the specified goals are being met?

_____

_____

_____

_____

_____

_____

- - - - - - - - - - - - - - - - - - - -

Your list should be similar to the one following:

Working with fellow students in group situations
Providing help to fellow students
Receiving help from fellow students
Talking quietly with fellow students
Hand-raising in response to questions
Sitting quietly and attentively when other students are talking
Sitting quietly and attentively when teacher is talking
Sitting quietly in seat when appropriate
Remaining with designated group during group activities
Studying at designated times
Working on homework
Contributing positively to group projects
Handing in homework on time
Completing good quality homework

7. Previously we divided the list of specific inappropriate behaviors into
categories and labeled each of the groupings, You should now do the same
thing for the list of appropriate behaviors. First, for practice, divide
into categories the list you generated. Then group into categories and label
the behaviors in our list, presented below.

Category Label	Behavior
	Working with fellow students
	Providing help to others
	Receiving help from others
	Talking quietly with others
	Hand-raising
	Sitting quietly and listening to other students
	Sitting quietly and listening to teacher
	Sitting quietly in seat
	Remaining with group
	Studying
	Working on homework
	Contributing positively to groups
	Handing in homework on time
	Completing good quality homework

- - - - - - - - - - - - - - - - -

Our groupings and the category labels for our list are presented below.

Category Label	Behavior
Social behaviors	Working with fellow students
	Providing help to others
	Receiving help from others
	Talking quietly with others

Category Label	Behavior
Classroom conduct	Sitting quietly and listening to other students
	Hand-raising
	Sitting quietly and listening to teacher
	Sitting quietly in seat
	Remaining with group
Work habits	Studying
	Working on homework
	Contributing positively to groups
	Handing in homework on time
	Completing good quality homework

For convenience, we will use these categories later as we work out a program for Herman.

SELECTING AN APPROACH
AND DESIGNING A DATA-RECORDING SYSTEM

Now we can proceed to the next step in implementing an applied Operant Learning Theory program for Herman: selecting a particular approach to use. This step is fairly complicated and should be broken down into several steps. The basic problem is that at this point a teacher may not have enough objective information about the nature and extent of the student's behavioral problems. For example, after reading the description of Herman's behavior, most of us might describe him (perhaps erroneously) as misbehaving "all the time." In fact, it is critical to know whether Herman is misbehaving all the time, since that fact would dictate the choice of an Operant Learning approach. If Herman is misbehaving all the time, no instances of positive behavior remain to be reinforced, and, therefore, the social-reinforcement and token-reinforcement approaches will be relatively useless. Such a situation would require the punishment combined with reinforcement approach to suppress the extreme frequency of inappropriate behaviors.

In addition, it is important to know the frequency of severe forms of misbehavior. If Herman endangers other students by hitting them or throwing objects at them with considerable regularity, we would again have to choose punishment as our approach for modifying Herman's behavior.

The above considerations point to a need for collecting data on the exact nature and regularity of a student's misbehavior before choosing an applied Operant Learning Theory approach. The collection of such data before implementing a program serves several purposes. First, it provides teachers with the information necessary for making an informed choice of the appropriate applied Operant Learning Theory approach. Second, it provides a standard of comparison which can be used to assess the effect of the program. For example, let's say that Herman is out of his seat approximately 50 percent of the time as we observe him before implementing the program. After several weeks of program implementation (during which you continue to collect data), you check the frequency of his out-of-seat behavior and discover that he is still out of his seat approximately 50 percent of the time. The decision is inescapable; the program is not working and changes have to be made. Alternatively, if his out-of-seat behavior has dropped off considerably from the preprogram level, you have concrete evidence that the program is effective.

The collection of student behavioral data also serves another purpose. It provides an objective picture of student behavior which is untainted by the emotional responses of the frustrated teacher. Teachers sometimes overreact to particular kinds of student behaviors, and this overreaction tends to distort their perceptions of everything a student does. For example, let's take the case of Billy Smith, the boy we described in the Introduction, who sneezed all the time. Perhaps Billy's teacher finds his sneezing particularly irritating so that this irritation tends to make her perceive everything Billy does in a negative light. In situations like this, evidence on the frequency and nature of appropriate and inappropriate behavior can help bring teacher perceptions into line with reality. Faced with concrete evidence, teachers sometimes decide that their own perceptions are at fault rather than the student's behavior. It is important to identify the existence of a real problem before applying Operant Learning Theory to correct it.

Having discussed some of the reasons why the collection of data is an essential component of any applied Operant Learning Theory program, we are now ready to design a data-collection procedure for Herman. First, we must design a data-recording form. The essential components for any data-recording form are: (1) a space for the student's name; (2) a space for the inclusive dates of the recording period; (3) spaces for listing the specific behaviors to be observed, and (4) spaces for recording the occurrence of each of the specified behaviors. An example of a general form for recording data, including each of these four components, is presented in Figure 1.

The form includes several other important details. This form would be used for an entire school week, so it is divided into the five days of the week. Under each of the weekdays are eight subdivisions, which are spaces for recording eight separate behavioral observations during each of the days. The actual number of behavioral observations to be taken in a given day can be flexible. The rule of thumb is that you should take enough observations to provide a stable picture of student behavior. For example, it would take quite a while to accumulate enough data to form a stable picture of a student's behavior if the behavior were observed only once a day. Having looked at the general format for a data-recording form, we can now design a form specifically for Herman.

---

8. Figure 2 illustrates a partially filled-in data-recording form for Herman. Your task is to complete the form. Refer back to answers 5 and 7 for the specific behaviors to list in the blanks.

- - - - - - - - - - - - - - - - - -

Figure 1. Data–Recording Form

Student Name _____   Recording Dates _____

DAYS

Behaviors Observed	MONDAY								TUESDAY								WEDNESDAY								THURSDAY								FRIDAY							
	1	2	3	4	5	6	7	8	1	2	3	4	5	6	7	8	1	2	3	4	5	6	7	8	1	2	3	4	5	6	7	8	1	2	3	4	5	6	7	8

Student Name ____Herman Bonham____ ____10/13/78 – 10/18/78____

Behavior Category	Positive or Negative	Specific Behaviors	Monday 1 2 3 4 5 6 7 8	Tuesday 1 2 3 4 5 6 7 8	Wednesday 1 2 3 4 5 6 7 8	Thursday 1 2 3 4 5 6 7 8	Friday 1 2 3 4 5 6 7 8
Social Behaviors	Negative Social Behaviors	Grabbing objects					
		Kicking					
		Hitting					
		Biting					
		Spitting					
	Positive Social Behaviors	Working with others					
		Providing help					
		Receiving help					
		Talking quietly					
Classroom Conduct	Negative Vocal Disruptions						
	Negative Physical Activity						
	Negative Noise with Objects						
	Positive Classroom Conduct						
Work Habits	Positive Work Habits						
	Quality and Frequency of Homework						

Figure 2. Partially Filled-in Data-Recording Form

Your form should look like the one in Figure 3.

The completed form (Figure 3) would be used to record Herman's behaviors for five days, with eight behavioral observations on each day. However, two of the items on our form ("Homework on time" and "Good quality homework") cannot be observed eight times a day. Therefore, for these two items we will simply check Column 8 on a given day if homework has been handled in that day and if the homework is of good quality.

Now that we have a data-recording form, we are ready to begin recording actual behavior. The following method might be used: Every thirty minutes (for a total of eight times per day) an observer would observe Herman's behavior for a thirty-second interval. During that thirty-second interval, the observer would check off each of the specified behaviors which occurred during the observation period. Notice that we speak of an observer, rather than the person teaching the class, doing the behavior recording. With a data-recording form as detailed as the one we have designed, a teacher would find it difficult to keep track of time, record behaviors, and teach, all at the same time. Unless the teacher could somehow be free for periodic intervals during the day to record behavior, we would recommend that the observing be done by a classroom aide or some other responsible adult.

We do not mean to suggest that a data-recording system cannot be designed for use in a classroom where the teacher is the only adult present. In that case, however, behaviors simply cannot be recorded in fine detail. For example, rather than recording the occurrence of specific behaviors, the teacher could set up a system to record the occurrence of categories of behavior. Thus, we could design a form to record the occurrence of antisocial behavior (as a category), negative classroom conduct, positive social and classroom behavior, and so on. With this kind of form, a teacher would have to record only four or five events per observation period and should be able to do so without assistance.

If at all possible, a data-recording system should be fairly detailed. The finely detailed approach provides a much more complete picture of student behavior than does an approach which collapses specific behaviors into broad categories. However, if the finely detailed approach is not possible, the category approach will still provide useful data for choosing the appropriate applied Operant Learning Theory program and evaluting the impact of the program.

Let's say that an observer recorded Herman's behavior for a week, following the procedure we just described (making eight thirty-second observations per day). The data-recording form for the week of observations appears in Figure 4.

The checkmarks in the columns signify that the behavior occurred during the observation interval. Notice that Herman handed in his homework on only one day (Thursday) and that he did not receive a mark for good quality for the entire week.

Now that we have a record of Herman's behavior for a week, the next step is to evaluate the data so that we can use them to make some decisions.

Figure 3. Completed Data-Recording Form

Student Name: Herman Bonham   10/13/78 - 10/18/78

Behavior Category	Positive or Negative	Specific Behaviors	Monday 1 2 3 4 5 6 7 8	Tuesday 1 2 3 4 5 6 7 8	Wednesday 1 2 3 4 5 6 7 8	Thursday 1 2 3 4 5 6 7 8	Friday 1 2 3 4 5 6 7 8
Social Behaviors	Negative Social Behaviors	Grabbing objects					
		Kicking					
		Hitting					
		Biting					
		Spitting					
	Positive Social Behaviors	Working with others					
		Providing help					
		Receiving help					
		Talking quietly					
Classroom Conduct	Negative Vocal Disruptions	Yelling comments at teacher					
		Yelling at other students					
		Coughing loudly					
		Making obscene noises					
		Whistling loudly					
	Negative Physical Activity	Out of seat w/o permission					
		Running					
		Jumping					
		Moving chairs					
	Negative Noise with Objects	Banging books					
		Tapping pencil					
		Hitting desk with hands					
	Positive Classroom Conduct	Hand-raising					
		Remaining with group					
		Sitting, listening to student					
		Sitting, listening to teacher					
		Sitting quietly in seat					
Work Habits	Positive Work Habits	Studying					
		Positive group contribution					
	Quality and Frequency of Homework	Working on homework					
		Homework on time					
		Good quality homework					

9. All of the information from the data-recording form (Figure 4) is condensed in Figure 5. Figure 5 lists the behavior categories, the specific behaviors, the number of observations per day (always eight on this form), the number of times the behavior was present during the eight observation intervals on a given day, and the percentage of intervals in which a particular behavior was observed. On Monday, for example, Herman was observed grabbing objects from other students during two (25 percent) of the eight observation intervals. You will notice that the table is only partially filled in. Your task is to complete the table. In some places we have already counted the number of intervals in which a behavior was present. You must still compute the percentage of intervals in which the behavior occurs. (The formula for percentage is: number of observations—always eight—divided into the number of intervals in which the behavior was present. For example, $2/8 = 0.25$, or 25 percent). In other places in the figure, you will have to go to the data-recording form (Figure 4) to count the number of observation intervals in which the behavior was present, and then compute the percentage of observation intervals in which the behavior was present. When you are finished, all of the blanks in Figure 5 should be filled in.

- - - - - - - - - - - - - - - - - -

Your completed figure should match Figure 6.

You should carefully look at the data in Figure 6. As you can see, several of the negative social behaviors occur with sufficiently high frequency to be of real concern. Also, a number of specific behaviors in the negative classroom conduct categories are occurring with a higher-than-desirable frequency. In contrast, most of the appropriate or positive behaviors are occurring with such low frequency that they are virtually nonexistent.

The data in Figure 6 can be condensed even further by combining specific behaviors into general categories.

10. Figure 7 is only partially completed, and your task will be to fill in the missing blanks. Again you will need to refer to the data-recording form (Figure 4) to complete the figure. Figure 7 can be completed by counting the number of observation intervals for a given day during which at least one specific behavior from a given category was observed. For example, on Monday, during five (63 percent) of the eight observation intervals, at least one behavior was observed which was contained in the negative social behavior category.

- - - - - - - - - - - - - - - - - -

Figure 4. Data-Recording Form after Week of Observation

Student Name: Herman Bonham — 10/13/78 – 10/18/78

Behavior Category		Specific Behaviors	Monday 1–8	Tuesday 1–8	Wednesday 1–8	Thursday 1–8	Friday 1–8
Social Behaviors	Negative Social Behaviors	Grabbing objects					
		Kicking					
		Hitting					
		Biting					
		Spitting					
	Positive Social Behaviors	Working with others					
		Providing help					
		Receiving help					
		Talking quietly					
	Negative Vocal Disruptions	Yelling comments at teacher					
		Yelling at other students					
		Coughing loudly					
		Making obscene noises					
		Whistling loudly					
Classroom Conduct	Negative Physical Activity	Out of seat w/o permission					
		Running					
		Jumping					
		Moving chairs					
	Negative Noise with Objects	Banging books					
		Tapping pencil					
		Hitting desk with hands					
	Positive Classroom Conduct	Hand-raising					
		Sitting, listening to student					
		Sitting, listening to teacher					
		Sitting quietly in seat					
		Remaining with group					
Work Habits	Positive Work Habits	Studying					
		Positive group contribution					
		Working on homework					
	Quality and Frequency of Homework	Homework on time					
		Good quality homework					

Figure 5.   Partially Filled-in Evaluation of Behavior Data

Behavior Category	Positive or Negat.	Specific Behaviors	Monday			Tuesday			Wednesday			Thursday			Friday		
			# Obs	Pres	%	# Obs	Pres	%	# Obs	Pres	%	# Obs	Pres	%	# Obs	Pres	%
Social Behaviors	Negative Social Behaviors	Grabbing objects	8	2	25	8	2	25	8	3	38	8	1	13	8	2	25
		Kicking	8	1	13	8	0	0	8	1	13	8	0	0	8	1	13
		Hitting	8	2	25	8	2	25	8	1	13	8	2	25	8	2	25
		Biting	8	0	0	8	0	0	8	0	0	8	0	0	8	0	0
		Spitting	8	1	13	8	1	13	8	1	13	8	1	13	8	1	25
	Positive Social Behaviors	Working with others	8	1	13	8	1	13	8	1	13	8	0	0	8	0	0
		Providing help	8	0	0	8	0	0	8	0	0	8	0	0	8	0	0
		Receiving help	8	0	0	8	0	0	8	0	0	8	1	13	8	1	13
		Talking quietly	8	0	0	8	0	0	8	1	13	8	0	0	8	0	0
	Negative Vocal	Yelling at teacher	8	1	13	8	1	13	8	1	13	8	1	13	8	1	13
		Yelling at students	8	2	25	8	3	28	8	3	38	8	4	50	8	2	25
		Coughing loudly	8	1	13	8	1	13	8	1	13	8	0	0	8	0	0
	Disruptions	Making obscene noises	8	2		8	3		8	0		8	1		8	1	
		Whistling loudly	8	0		8	1		8	2		8	0		8	1	
Classroom Conduct	Negative Physical Activity	Out of seat	8	4		8	4		8	3		8	4		8	4	
		Running	8	0		8	1		8	1		8	1		8	0	
		Jumping	8	0		8	0		8	0		8	1		8	0	
		Moving chairs	8	1		8	0		8	1		8	0		8	0	
	Negative Noise w/ Objects	Banging books	8			8			8			8					
		Tapping pencil	8			8			8			8					
		Hitting hands on desk	8			8			8			8					
	Positive Classroom Conduct	Hand-raising	8			8			8			8					
		Sitting, listening to student	8															
		Sitting, listening to teacher																
		Sitting quietly in seat																
		Remaining with group																
Work Habits	Positive Work Habits	Studying																
		Positive group contributions																
		Working on homework																

Behavior Category	Positive or Negat.	Specific Behaviors	Monday			Tuesday			Wednesday			Thursday			Friday		
			# Obs	# Pres	%	# Obs	# Pres	%	# Obs	# Pres	%	# Obs	# Pres	%	# Obs	# Pres	%
Social Behaviors	Negative Social Behaviors	Grabbing objects	8	2	25	8	2	25	8	3	38	8	1	13	8	3	38
		Kicking	8	1	13	8	0	0	8	1	13	8	0	0	8	1	13
		Hitting	8	2	25	8	2	25	8	1	13	8	2	25	8	2	25
		Biting	8	0	0	8	0	0	8	0	0	8	0	0	8	2	25
		Spitting	8	1	13	8	1	13	8	1	13	8	1	13	8	2	25
	Positive Social Behaviors	Working with others	8	1	13	8	1	13	8	1	13	8	0	0	8	0	0
		Providing help	8	0	0	8	0	0	8	0	0	8	0	0	8	0	0
		Receiving help	8	0	0	8	0	0	8	0	0	8	1	13	8	1	13
Classroom Conduct	Negative Vocal Disruptions	Talking quietly	8	0	0	8	0	0	8	1	13	8	0	0	8	0	0
		Yelling at teacher	8	1	13	8	1	13	8	1	13	8	1	13	8	1	13
		Yelling at students	8	2	25	8	3	38	8	3	38	8	4	50	8	2	25
		Coughing loudly	8	1	13	8	1	13	8	1	13	8	1	13	8	0	0
		Making obscene noises	8	2	25	8	3	38	8	1	13	8	1	13	8	1	13
		Whistling loudly	8	0	0	8	1	13	8	2	25	8	0	0	8	1	13
	Negative Physical Activity	Out of seat	8	4	50	8	4	**50**	8	3	38	8	4	50	8	4	50
		Running	8	0	0	8	1	13	8	1	13	8	1	13	8	0	0
		Jumping	8	0	0	8	0	0	8	0	0	8	1	13	8	0	0
		Moving chairs	8	1	13	8	0	0	8	1	13	8	0	0	8	0	0
	Negative Noise w/ Objects	Banging books	8	1	13	8	2	25	8	1	13	8	1	13	8	1	13
		Tapping pencil	8	1	13	8	0	0	8	0	0	8	1	13	8	0	0
		Hitting hands on desk	8	0	0	8	1	13	8	0	0	8	1	13	8	0	0
	Positive Classroom Conduct	Hand-raising	8	0	0	8	0	0	8	0	0	8	1	13	8	0	0
		Sitting, listening to student	8	0	0	8	1	13	8	0	0	8	1	13	8	0	0
		Sitting, listening to teacher	8	1	13	8	0	0	8	0	0	8	1	13	8	0	0
		Sitting quietly in seat	8	0	0	8	1	13	8	1	13	8	1	13	8	1	13
		Remaining with group	8	0	0	8	0	0	8	1	13	8	0	0	8	0	0
Work Habits	Positive Work Habits	Studying	8	0	0	8	1	13	8	1	13	8	0	0	8	0	0
		Positive group contributions	8	1	13	8	0	0	8	1	13	8	0	0	8	0	13
		Working on homework	8	1	13	8	0	0	8	0	0	8	1	13	8	2	25

Figure 6. Completed Evaluation of Behavior Data

Figure 7. Partially Filled-in Categorization of Behaviors

Behavior category	Monday			Tuesday			Wednesday			Thursday			Friday		
	# Obs	Pres	%	# Obs	Pres	%	# Obs	Pres	%	# Obs	Pres	%	# Obs	Pres	%
Negative social behaviors	8	5	63	8	5	63	8	5	63	8	4	50	8	4	50
Negative classroom conduct	8	6	75	8	6	75	8	6		8	6		8	5	
Positive social behaviors	8			8			8			8			8		
Positive classroom conduct															
Positive work habits															

Your completed Figure 7 should be the same as Figure 8.

The final step in reducing the data from the data-recording form is to graph the results. Putting the results in graph form makes it very easy to check the frequency with which given categories of behavior are occurring.

11. Below we have presented two graphs which give us a picture of the frequency of Herman's appropriate and inappropriate behavior. The graphs were drawn using the data presented in Figure 8. For example, instances of negative social behaviors were observed in 63 percent of the observation intervals on Monday, Tuesday, and Wednesday, and in 50 percent of the observation intervals on Thursday and Friday. ·

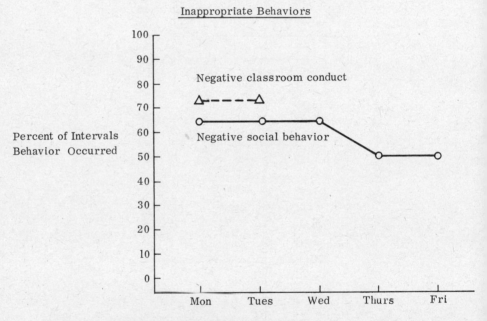

Inappropriate Behaviors

Notice that the graph is incomplete in that three of the points for the negative classroom conduct category remain to be filled in. Your task is to fill in the missing points.

Figure 8. Categorization of Behaviors

Behavior category	Monday			Tuesday			Wednesday			Thursday			Friday		
	# Obs	Pres	%	# Obs	Pres	%	# Obs	Pres	%	# Obs	Pres	%	# Obs	Pres	%
Negative social behaviors	8	5	63	8	5	63	8	5	63	8	5	40	8	4	50
Negative classroom conduct	8	6	75	8	6	75	8	6	75	8	6	75	8	5	63
Positive social behaviors	8	1	13	8	1	13	8	2	25	8	1	13	8	1	13
Positive classroom conduct	8	1	13	8	2	25	8	1	13	8	1	13	8	1	13
Positive work habits	8	2	25	8	1	13	8	1	13	8	2	25	8	2	25

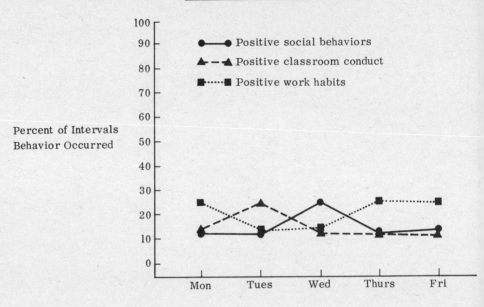

Appropriate Behaviors

Your graph should be identical to the one below:

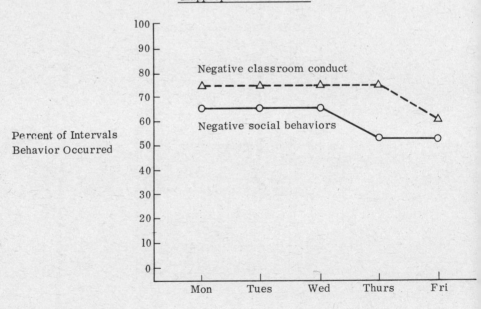

Inappropriate Behaviors

We have now completed the necessary steps leading to a decision about which applied Operant Learning Theory approach to use. Through our data-collection process, we have obtained a rather complete picture of Herman's behavior. We know that he was acting inappropriately in the classroom between 63 percent and 75 percent of the times he was observed. We also know that he was engaging in negative social behaviors between 50 and 63 percent of the times he was observed. On the positive behavior side, his frequencies of positive work habits, positive classroom conduct, and positive social behavior are all low, ranging from 10 percent to 25 percent of the times he was observed.

These results suggest that it might be useful to try a mix of two applied Operant Learning Theory approaches with Herman. First, since several of Herman's negative social behaviors are both severe and frequent (he was hitting fellow students as frequently as 38 percent of the times observed), steps should be taken to eliminate them as rapidly as possible.

12. What applied Operant Learning Theory approach would you use to reduce the frequency of Herman's severe anti-social behavior?

_____

_____

_____

Punishment combined with reinforcement.

The remainder of Herman's behavior problems (those involving classroom conduct) are not as severe as his anti-social behavior, and another Operant Learning approach would be most appropriate for these problems.

13. What applied Operant Learning Theory approach would you choose to reduce the frequency of Herman's negative classroom conduct behaviors and to increase the frequency of Herman's positive work habits, positive classroom conduct, and positive social behaviors?

_____

_____

_____

_____

The most reasonable approach would be social reinforcement of appropriate behaviors combined with ignoring his negative classroom conduct behavior. Ultimately, we want Herman's behavior to be responsive to social reinforcement. At this point we have no evidence that Herman is unresponsive to teacher-delivered social reinforcement. So we will first try social reinforcement and, if he proves to be unresponsive to social reinforcement, we can then move to the stronger token-reinforcement approach.

DEVELOPING AND EXPLAINING CLASSROOM RULES

A set of classroom rules should speicify the behaviors which the teacher considers to be undesirable and, if a punishment approach is used, how punishment will be administered. One useful approach when working with a single misbehaving student such as Herman is to design a behavioral contract. A behavioral contract is an agreement which specifies desirable and undesirable classroom behaviors and any special consequences associated with performing any of the undesirable behaviors. The contract is signed by both the teacher and the student and often by the student's parents.

An example of a behavioral contract which we might draw up for Herman is presented in Figure 9.

Figure 9. Behavior Contract

Behavior Contract

between

Herman Bonham, you (the teacher)

and Mr. and Mrs. Bonham

The goal of this contract is to reduce the number of times Herman is misbehaving and to increase the number of times Herman is behaving as he should in the classroom. Herman should not misbehave in the following ways:

Mistreating Others

a. Do not hit, kick, bite, spit at, or throw objects at other students.
b. Do not pick up or grab objects which are not yours without permission.

Since these behaviors are dangerous and someone could be hurt by them, a special punishment will be given if Herman does these things. The first time he does any one of these things, he will receive a warning. The second time he does one of these things, he will be removed from the classroom and left by himself for ten minutes.

Disrupting the Classroom

a. Do not talk or yell out in the classroom when you are not supposed to.
b. Do not make loud or offensive noises which bother the class or
   the teacher.
c. Do not leave your seat when you are supposed to be in it.
d. Do not make noises with objects or your hands or feet which
   bother the teacher or other students.

Rather than doing the above things, Herman should be doing the
things below.

Treating Others Well

a. Work with others, provide help to others, and receive help from
   others.
b. Talk quietly with others when it is appropriate to do so.

Practicing Good Classroom Conduct

a. Raise your hand when you have something to say.
b. Stay in your seat when you are supposed to.
c. Listen when the teacher or someone else is talking.

Practicing Good Work Habits

a. Study in class during study periods.
b. Work on homework when you are supposed to and hand in your
   homework on time.
c. Be helpful when you are working on projects with others.

Signed: _____   _____
            Herman Bonham   (the teacher)

        _____   _____
            Mr. Bonham   Mrs. Bonham

Having drawn up a behavioral contract, the teacher should sit down with
the student (and, in our sample contract, the parents) and explain the contract
to make sure every item is clearly understood.

In a situation where more than one student is the focus of the applied
Operant Learning Theory program, the procedure for formulating classroom
rules (except for the behavioral contract) would be similar to our example
above. The desirable and undesirable behaviors would be identified and made
explicit. They would then be explained to all students involved. Periodic
reviews of the classroom rules will keep them fresh in the students' minds.

SYSTEMATICALLY APPLYING THE RULES:
IMPLEMENTING AND EVALUATING THE
APPLIED OPERANT LEARNING THEORY PROGRAM

We have now completed all of the preliminary steps before we actually implement an applied Operant Learning Theory program. As a review, fill in the missing information in the following question.

14. List the four steps which must be completed before actual implementation of an applied Operant Learning Theory program.

1. _____

_____

2. _____

_____

3. _____

_____

4. _____

_____

- -

1. State the goals of the applied Operant Learning Theory program.
2. Select the specific inappropriate behaviors which should be decreased in frequency and the specific appropriate behaviors which should be increased in frequency.
3. Select an applied Operant Learning Theory approach to use. This step involves designing a behavior recording form, collecting preimplementation (baseline) data, and reducing and graphing that data.
4. Formulate and explain the classroom rules.

We have decided that we will use a punishment combined with reinforcement approach to reduce the frequency of Herman's socially abusive behavior and a social reinforcement approach for the remainder of Herman's behavior. These two approaches could be implemented by following the procedures below.

Punish socially abusive behavior. Herman should be warned upon the occurrence of his first socially abusive act on a given day. If a socially abusive act is repeated during that day, he will be removed from the classroom (an environment where he has access to reinforcers) and placed by himself in an uninteresting environment for ten minutes. The type of uninteresting environment a punished child is placed in can vary as a function of the resources available in a school. Some schools have set up special "time-out" rooms in which to place recalcitrant students. In other schools a student might more appropriately be sent to sit in a school office under the watchful eye of an adult. The critical aspect of a choice of punishment location is that the location must not provide sources of reinforcement for the student. If the location does provide sources of reinforcement, the child may find the punishment location more desirable than the classroom. In such a case, by sending a student to the punishment location, you could be encouraging the very behavior you wish to discourage.

Ignore inappropriate classroom conduct. Whenever Herman engages in inappropriate classroom conduct, he should be ignored. The assumption behind this rule is that students have a reason for behaving inappropriately in class. Most frequently, the reason is to gain the attention of the teacher or other students. When we ignore inappropriate behavior we are withholding attention (withholding reinforcement), and we know that behavior not followed by reinforcement should decline in frequency. To enlist the assistance of other students in the classroom is often useful in this situation. The teacher could explain to the other students that everyone should attempt to help a misbehaving student improve his or her behavior, and one way to do so is to ignore the student when misbehavior occurs.

Provide social reinforcement for appropriate behavior. Catch Herman being good, then reinforce him. Reinforcement could take a variety of forms, such as verbal praise (that is, "You're working very well now, Herman," or "Thank you for raising your hand"), a pat on the back, or a simple smile. In the early stages of the program, social reinforcement should be delivered as often as possible. Then, after the target behaviors have shown an improvement and have leveled off, reinforcement can be provided more intermittently.

Let us now jump ahead in time. The program has been in effect for three weeks. Herman has been punished by removing him from the classroom when he is abusive towards other students, and his negative classroom conduct has been ignored. In addition, his positive social behaviors, positive classroom conduct, and his positive work habits have been socially reinforced whenever they occurred. During this three-week period we have continued to collect data using the data-recording form. The percentage of category behaviors are presented in Figure 10. These percentages are the end product of the same observation and data-collection procedure which was followed earlier.

Figure 10. Percentage of Observation Periods
In Which Specified Behavior Occurred

Behavior category	Week One					Week Two					Week Three				
	M	T	W	Th	F	M	T	W	Th	F	M	T	W	Th	F
Negative social behaviors	63	50	50	38	38	25	38	25	25	13	13	13	0	13	0
Negative classroom conduct	63	75	63	50	63	50	50	38	50	63	50	38	38	50	38
Positive social behaviors	0	13	13	25	13	13	0	13	13	13	25	13	25	25	13
Positive classroom conduct	13	25	13	0	13	13	0	13	0	0	13	25	13	25	13
Positive work habits	25	13	25	25	13	25	38	25	13	25	38	25	25	13	25

15. Below are the graphs for the baseline period before we implemented our program, along with space for plotting the data gathered during the next three weeks. We have plotted the negative social behavior and the negative classroom conduct data for the first week of our implementation program. Using Figure 10, complete the graphs.

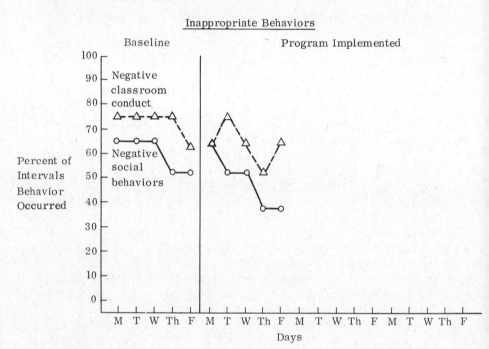

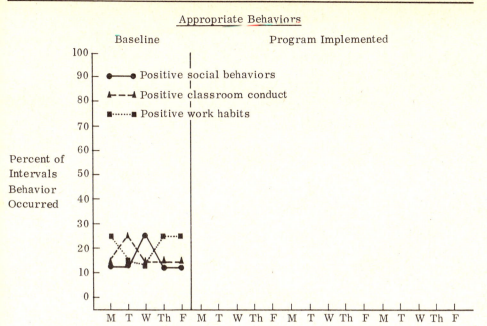

Appropriate Behaviors

Your graphs should be identical to the ones below:

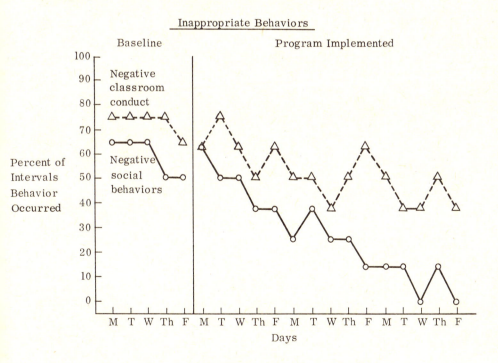

Inappropriate Behaviors

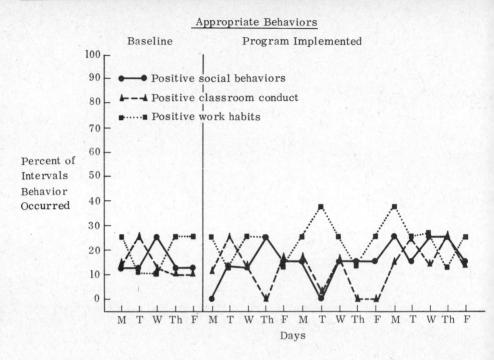

16. After examining the graph for inappropriate behaviors, what would you conclude about the effectiveness of the program in <u>reducing negative classroom conduct</u>?

_____

_____

_____

_____

- - - - - - - - - - - - - - - - - -

The program seems to be having some impact on negative classroom conduct, since the frequency of inappropriate behaviors in this category has dropped off somewhat. However, behaviors in this category are still at a higher-than-desirable level.

17. After examining the graph for inappropriate behaviors, what would you conclude about the effectiveness of the program in <u>reducing negative social</u> behaviors?

_____

_____

- - - - - - - - - - - - - - - - -

The data indicate that the program has been highly successful in reducing the incidence of negative social behaviors. The frequency of these behaviors has been reduced from about 58 percent in the baseline period to about 7 percent in the last week of program implementation.

18. After examining the graph for appropriate behaviors, what would you conclude about the effectiveness of the program in increasing the rate of positive work habits, social behaviors, and classroom conduct?

- - - - - - - - - - - - - - - - -

The program appears to be a failure in increasing the rate of positive behaviors. Virtually no evidence suggests that the rate of these behaviors is increasing.

We have a mixed verdict in evaluating the success of the program at this point. The program is highly successful in reducing the incidence of negative social behaviors and appears to be having some impact on negative classroom conduct. However, the positive behavior aspects of the program are a complete failure. No evidence suggests that the frequency of positive behaviors has increased.

19. Imagine you are Herman's teacher. When faced with this situation, what would you do now?

- - - - - - - - - - - - - - - - -

You should change Operant Learning approaches. Obviously providing social reinforcement for appropriate behavior is not having an impact on Herman's behavior. The next logical step is to try a token-reinforcement approach. Token reinforcement works with many students who are not responsive to social reinforcement delivered by the teacher. Herman's unresponsiveness to social reinforcement for appropriate behavior is probably also influencing his frequency of negative classroom conduct behaviors. One certain way to reduce negative classroom behavior is to increase the frequency of positive classroom behaviors. A student cannot simultaneously be doing something appropriate and something inappropriate. Therefore, if we can find an effective reinforcer for increasing Herman's frequency of positive classroom conduct, we will also be very likely to reduce his frequency of negative classroom conduct.

Instituting a token-reinforcement approach would involve the following steps. First, you would have to generate a tangible reward "menu" (see Chapter 1). Herman would exchange his accumulated tokens for items on this menu. The menu could be generated by sitting down with Herman and finding out what objects he would like to have or what activities he would like to do (within reason and available resources) in exchange for accumulated tokens. After generating a list, you then establish an exchange rate. For example, an extra ten minutes of recess or the opportunity to be a street guard for a day might be exchanged for fifty accumulated tokens. In conjunction with the parents, other, more valued items, such as a new record or a ticket to a local football game, might be exchanged for 100 tokens.

After developing the menu and an exchange system, your next step would be to develop a procedure for dispensing tokens and to explain that procedure to Herman. Among the many possibilities for dispensing tokens are poker chips, initialed squares of paper and so on, but the simplest is probably to tape on the corner of Herman's desk a tablet which has been lined off into small squares. You would then explain to Herman that for every ten minutes he is obeying the classroom rules, you will initial two of the squares on the tablet. In addition, you tell Herman that if he has done something wrong during that ten minute period, you will take away (erase) two of the squares.

20. We have just developed a procedure for implementing a token-reinforcement system. Recall Chapter 1. What one other thing should we be sure to do when we are giving a token reinforcement to Herman?

_____

_____

_____

_____

- -

We should always remember to provide social reinforcement at the same time that we are giving token reinforcement, since we want to get rid of the token system as quickly as possible. By repeatedly pairing social reinforcement and token reinforcement, social reinforcement will, over time, take on stronger reinforcing properties. This change allows us eventually to phase out the token system and replace it with a social-reinforcement system.

Let us assume that we have implemented our token system in place of the social-reinforcement system and that we have left the rest of the program the same. Two weeks have passed, and we have added the latest two weeks' worth of data to our previous graphs. The graphs appear below.

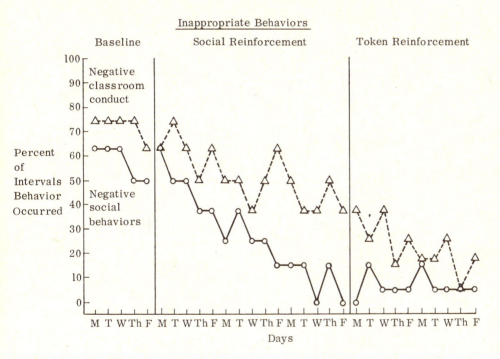

Inappropriate Behaviors

Appropriate Behaviors

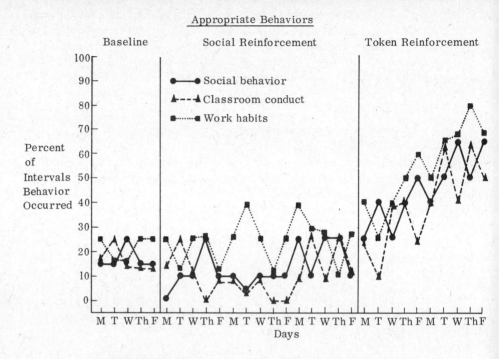

21. After examining the graphs, what is your conclusion about the effectiveness of the program?

- - - - - - - - - - - - - - - - - - -

Herman's level of inappropriate classroom conduct has dropped off to reasonable levels, and his incidence of positive behaviors has increased considerably.

The final stage in our program for Herman would be to phase out the token-reinforcement part of the procedure and to substitute naturally occurring reinforcers to maintain the effected behavior changes. As mentioned previously, social reinforcement should be given at the same time as token reinforcements are delivered. After the desired and undesired behaviors have reached stable levels, the teacher should continue to deliver social reinforcement at a high rate while reducing the frequency of token reinforcement. For example, rather than giving five tokens for every ten minutes of appropriate behavior, the teacher could give two tokens for ten minutes of appropriate behavior. The teacher could then give two tokens for twenty minutes of appropriate behavior, and then two tokens for sixty minutes, and so on, until the token system is phased out entirely. Careful monitoring of the behavioral levels should be maintained during this phasing out period to assure that the frequency of target behaviors does not drop or increase from the desired stable levels.

ADDITIONAL COMMENTS

Before we explore our next learning theory, several additional comments should be made about our coverage of applied Operant Learning Theory. At some points in our discussion of this theory, we have abbreviated our elaboration of certain critical points or steps. For example, in working through our example with Herman, we included a single week of baseline data. To obtain a truly stable picture of student behavior, the baseline period should be extended to several weeks. Our discussion of phasing out a token-reinforcement system was also necessarily abbreviated.

If you intend to use this type of system, you should examine one or more of the additional readings listed at the end of this chapter in order to become familiar with the subtleties and potential pitfalls associated with phasing out a token-reinforcement system.

Finally, if you believe that applied Operant Learning Theory is a useful addition to your repertoire of teaching tools, we encourage you to gain some practical experience in applying this theory before trying it out in your classroom. Many universities and colleges provide courses in applying Operant Learning Theory, and you might like to take advantage of the opportunity to gain supervised experience before you try it on your own.

ADDITIONAL READINGS

Cohen, H. L., and Filipczak, J. A New Learning Environment. San Francisco: Jossey-Bass, Inc., 1971.

Dollar, B. Humanizing Classroom Discipline. New York: Harper & Row, 1972.

Givner, A., and Graubard, P. S. A Handbook of Behavior Modification for the Classroom. New York: Holt, Rinehart and Winston, Inc., 1974.

Gnagy, W. J. Maintaining Discipline in Classroom Instruction. New York: Macmillan, 1975.

Macmillan, D. L. Behavior Modification in Education. New York: Macmillan, 1973.

Meacham, M. L., and Wiesen, A. E. Changing Classroom Behavior: A Manual for Precision Teaching. Scranton, Pennsylvania: International Textbook Co., 1970.

Mink, O. G. The Behavior Change Process. New York: Harper & Row, 1970.

Sulzer-Azaroff, B., and Mayer, G. R. Applying Behavior Analysis Procedures with Children and Youth. New York: Holt, Rinehart and Winston, Inc., 1977.

SELF-TEST

This self-test is designed to show you whether or not you have mastered the objectives of Chapter 2. Answer each question to the best of your ability, based on what you learned in this chapter. Correct answers are given following the test.

Read the following paragraph. Then answer the following questions that refer to the situation.

Mr. Cee, a sixth grade teacher, is concerned about Bill Boneau, a boy in his class. Bill, a natural leader, can command the respect of his fellow students. However, far too often, he uses this leadership ability to distract students from academics. In addition, he seldom pays attention to the teacher presentations or class discussions, and his homework is seldom done—all of which seem to be affecting his test scores. A notable exception to his lack of interest is science. Bill is interested in scientific projects, and he does well on them. His interest and leadership in this area have carried the entire class to levels of scientific inquiry and understanding far beyond those of any of Mr. Cee's previous classes.

1. List three inappropriate behaviors of Bill's which should be reduced in frequency.

    a. _____

    b. _____

    c. _____

2. List two appropriate behaviors to be encouraged.

    a. _____

    b. _____

3. List the rules for Bill that would be included in a behavioral contract.

    _____

    _____

    _____

    _____

    _____

4. Based on your conception of Bill as a student in a sixth grade class, fill
   in the following chart. Assume that you have observed him five times a
   day for each day of a school week. Check each behavior that existed each
   time he was observed. (Because you are imagining, there will be no
   "correct" answer. Your chart should reflect the general behavior pattern
   you would expect to observe.)

Student Name: Bill Boneau																									Dates: 5/2/79—5/6/79
Behavior	Period of Observation																								
	Monday					Tuesday					Wednesday					Thursday					Friday				
	1	2	3	4	5	1	2	3	4	5	1	2	3	4	5	1	2	3	4	5	1	2	3	4	5
Distracting students (−)																									
Not paying attention (−)																									
Not doing homework (−)																									
Being a helpful leader (+)																									
Contributing to science and other lessons (+)																									

5. Assume you have chosen to use the social-reinforcement technique. The
   graphs on the following page indicate the baseline data collected before
   implementing the program and for the first three weeks after implementing the program. Examine the graphs and then answer the questions that
   follow.

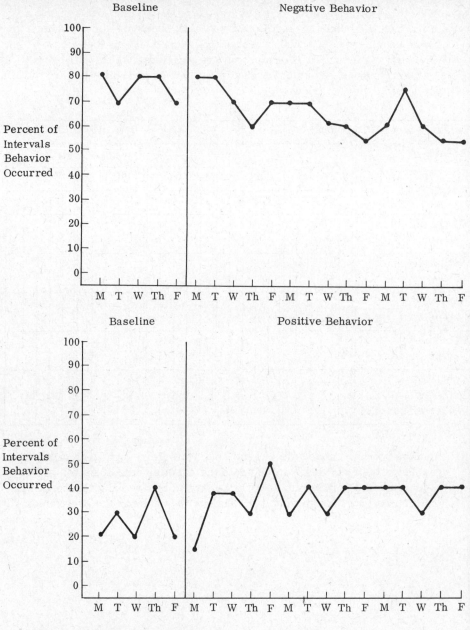

a. Is the program working? _____

b. What should you do next? _____

6. Assume you have instituted a token-economy system. Record the charted data on the graphs which follow:

Behavior	Week One					Week Two					Week Three				
Category	M	T	W	Th	F	M	T	W	Th	F	M	T	W	Th	F
Negative	70	60	70	50	40	50	40	30	30	20	40	20	10	20	10
Positive	20	30	20	40	30	40	40	60	60	70	60	80	90	50	60

Negative Behavior

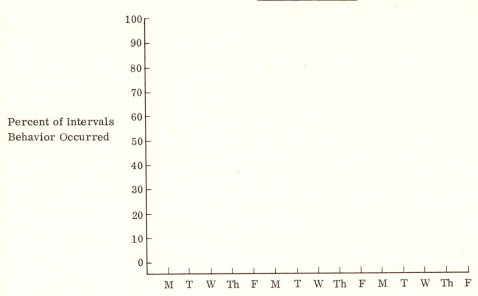

Positive Behavior

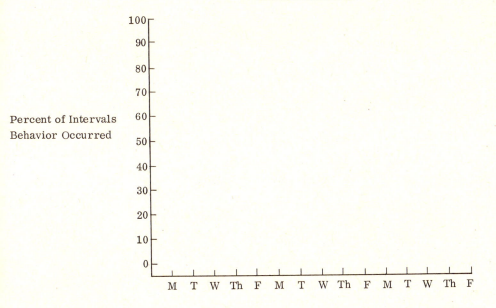

ANSWERS TO SELF-TEST

Compare your answers to the questions on the self-test with the answers given below. If all of your answers are correct, you are ready to go on to the next chapter. If you missed any questions, review the appropriate parts of the chapter before you go on.

1. a. Distracts fellow students
    b. Does not pay attention in class
    c. Seldom does homework

2. a. Displays leadership
    b. Exhibits interest in science

3. Bill will not:

    a. distract fellow students from teacher presentation and discussions.
    b. lead students to activities that interfere with their classroom work.

    He will:

    a. pay attention in class.
    b. Do his homework on time.
    c. help lead students toward academically related activities.

4. No "correct" answer can be given for the number or placement of checks. However, your chart should be similar to the one below. The "homework" category will be checked once each day if Bill has not done his homework; if he has done it, the box will remain empty.

Student Name: Bill Boneau										Dates: 5/2/79—5/6/79														
Behavior	Period of Observation																							
	Monday					Tuesday					Wednesday					Thursday					Friday				
	1	2	3	4	5	1	2	3	4	5	1	2	3	4	5	1	2	3	4	5	1	2	3	4	5
Distracting students (−)	✓	✓	✓		✓	✓	✓	✓	✓	✓	✓	✓			✓			✓	✓			✓	✓	✓	
Not paying attention (−)	✓	✓	✓	✓		✓			✓	✓			✓	✓		✓	✓		✓	✓	✓	✓	✓		
Not doing homework (−)			✓					✓					✓											✓	
Being a helpful leader (+)								✓										✓							
Contributing to science and other lessons (+)									✓				✓			✓									✓

5.　a. Not very well.
　　b. Try a token economy.

6.

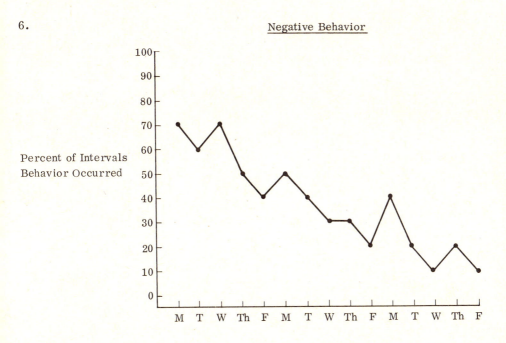

Negative Behavior

Percent of Intervals Behavior Occurred

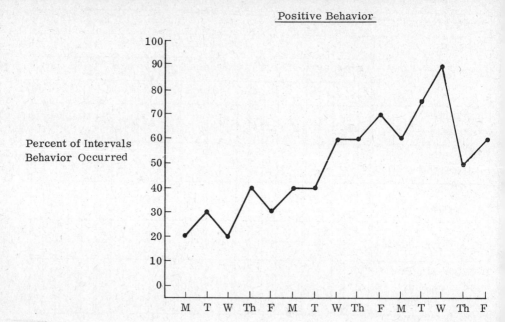

Positive Behavior

Percent of Intervals
Behavior Occurred

PART TWO
Associative Learning Theory

CHAPTER THREE
Principles of Associative Learning Theory for Classroom Use

In Chapters 1 and 2, we discussed how applied Operant Learning Theory was particularly useful in altering a student's behavior so that he or she is <u>prepared</u> to learn. In Chapters 3 and 4, we will discuss Associative Learning Theory, which focuses on the question of how to <u>present instruction</u> so that optimum learning occurs.

Associative Learning Theory is based on several assumptions about how people learn. Basic to these assumptions are the concepts of <u>stimulus</u> and <u>response.</u> A <u>stimulus</u> is any event which is perceived by the human sense receptors. A stimulus could be a visual event, a sound, a taste, a smell, a touch, or any combination of these. A <u>response</u> is any event or process which is elicited by (or results from) a stimulus. Some responses are purely reflexive (innate) in nature. For example, when we touch a hot stove, we perceive a stimulus, pain, and we automatically respond by jerking our hand away. Other responses develop as a function of learning. As an example, when we are asked what 9 times 6 (the stimulus) is, we give the response, 54. Clearly we have learned to give the response, 54, in the presence of the stimulus, "What is 9 times 6?"

Associative Learning Theory is based on the assumption that learning involves formation of "associative bonds" between stimulus and response events. These stimulus and response bonds are formed as a function of pairing both the stimulus and the response event in time. For example, we have learned to say, "54," in response to "What is 9 times 6?" because we have seen or heard both events presented together many times. The pairing of two events in time is called <u>contiguity.</u> Two events are contiguous if they occur together. Therefore, an associative bond is formed between two events when they are contiguous to one another. We have formed an associative bond between 9 times 6 and 54, because they have repeatedly been contiguous with one another.

This chapter shows how Associative Learning Theory can help us to increase the likelihood that associative bonds are formed between relevant instructional events. We will also discuss how to decrease the likelihood that events will weaken or interfere with already established associative bonds. After completing this chapter you should be able to:

1. Identify the type of educational situation or problem where Associative Learning Theory is most useful.
2. Specify the basic assumptions underlying Associative Learning Theory.
3. State each of the principles upon which Associative Learning Theory is based.
4. List the four steps required to implement an Associative Learning Theory approach to an educational problem.

SITUATIONS WHERE ASSOCIATIVE LEARNING THEORY IS RELEVANT

In the Introduction to this book, we described three kinds of educational problem situations which teachers frequently encounter: (1) situations where performance of inappropriate behaviors or failure to perform appropriate behaviors mean that the student is unprepared to benefit from educational experiences; (2) situations where the lack of critical basic skills prevents the student from benefiting from instruction; and (3) situations where the lack of complex cognitive skills prevents the student from benefiting from instruction. We have seen that applied Operant Learning Theory provides a useful approach for dealing with the first of these problem situations. Associative Learning Theory provides a useful approach for dealing with the second type of situation.

For Associative Learning Theory to be a reasonable approach, the situation to which it is to be applied should reflect two characteristics. First, the basic skill or skills which are lacking must be clearly definable and measurable. Second, the desired terminal skill must be clearly definable and measurable. As an example, let's say that one of your students is having considerable difficulty in solving long division problems. The ability to solve long division problems is a terminal skill which is readily measurable simply by giving the student a series of problems to solve. You can thus determine whether the student can solve the problems, and the particular basic skills which may be lacking can also be easily specified. Solving long division problems involves subskills such as the ability to multiply or subtract. By determining if the student can perform the subskills, you can isolate the subskill which is lacking and focus instruction on that skill. Mastery of the subskill should then lead to successful performance of the terminal skill.

---

1. Mr. Meyers teaches an automobile repair class in the local high school. Part of the instruction in the class focuses on the acquisition of "troubleshooting" skills. Troubleshooting an automobile involves carefully following a checklist of specified tests. The student must find a particular mechanical or electrical problem and repair it. Henry Fonzie, one of the students in Mr. Meyers' class, is having difficulty with this part of the class. Might Associative Learning Theory be useful in this situation? Explain.

— — — — — — — — — — — — — — — —

Yes, it might. Poor performance in troubleshooting means either that Henry is not performing some of the tests, that he is performing them out of sequence, or that he has difficulty repairing certain problems. These basic skills (performing and sequencing tests and repairing specific problems) can be clearly defined and measured. In addition, the desired terminal skill can be clearly defined and measured by giving Henry a car with a problem to see whether he can find the problem and fix it.

2. Ms. Moss teaches an advanced art class in a nearby high school. The students in her class are all reasonably competent technically, but, in her opinion, they display an appalling lack of creativity. Her students produce rather bland and traditional paintings, and she would like to teach them how to be more creative. Would Associative Learning Theory be helpful in this situation? Why?

_____

_____

_____

— — — — — — — — — — — — — — — —

No. In this situation we cannot define and measure the lack of subskills which may be responsible for the uncreative paintings. In addition, we cannot define or measure the desired terminal skill. A painting which Ms. Moss considers to be highly creative might be evaluated very differently by another viewer.

BASIC PRINCIPLES
UNDERLYING ASSOCIATIVE LEARNING THEORY

As noted earlier, Associative Learning Theory is based on the assumption that learning involves the formation of associative bonds between stimulus events and response events which occur contiguously in time. Five basic principles govern the formation and dissolution of associative bonds. Let us look at the first three principles.

Associative bonds increase in strength as a function of repeated pairings of stimulus and response events. The first principle simply means that the more often we have experienced a stimulus and response event together, the more likely that upon encountering the stimulus we will be able to provide the response. Multiplication tables and the alphabet are examples of stimulus and response bonds all of us learned in our own educational careers.

Associative bonds decrease in strength as a function of disuse. This second principle is based on common sense. If we learn something and do not use that learning for a long period of time, it is difficult to remember what we originally learned. As an example, about seventeen years ago one of the authors of this text had a reasonably good mastery of Japanese, and the other had reasonable facility with French. After many years of not using the languages, however, much of the ability to speak and understand Japanese and French has been lost.

The third principle underlying Associative Learning Theory states: Once associative bonds have been acquired, they can influence the learning of subsequent associative bonds. This influence can be positive, where prior learning makes subsequent learning easier; neutral, where prior learning has no effect on subsequent learning; or negative, where prior learning interfers with or inhibits subsequent learning. Previously acquired associative bonds can facilitate subsequent learning when both the stimulus and the response events are similar in both. For example, in learning a language such as French, some English and French words which are similar in spelling also have similar meanings:

French	English
amplitude	amplitude
camarade	comrade
parfait	perfect

In this case, knowing the English words should make it easier to learn the French words.

Prior learning has a neutral effect on subsequent learning (that is, neither facilitates nor inhibits it) when the stimulus and the response events differ in both prior and subsequent learning. Again using French as an example, the learning of French words which look different from English words should be unaffected by prior knowledge of English. Some examples of these words are:

French	English
mal de mer	seasick
ivre	drunk
gateau	cake

Knowing the English words above should have no effect on subsequent learning of the French words.

Prior learning can inhibit or interfere with subsequent learning when the stimulus events are similar but the response events are different. For example some French words which appear similar to English words but have different meanings:

French	English
rester	remain (looks like rest)
occasion	opportunity
hôtel de ville	town hall

In the above examples, knowing the English word and its meaning should make it more difficult to learn the French word.

---

3. Listed below are three French words and their English equivalents. For each word, decide if knowing the English word will facilitate, neutrally affect, or interfere with learning the French word.

French	English	
a. place	town square	_____
b. raifort ·	horseradish	_____
c. papier	paper	_____

- - - - - - - - - - - - - - - -

a. interfere with; b. neutral; c. facilitate.

The fourth principle underlying Associative Learning Theory states: Just as previously learned associative bonds can affect subsequent learning, <u>subsequent learning can affect the retention of previous learning.</u> If stimulus and response events are similar, subsequently learned associative bonds will facilitate the retention of previously acquired associative bonds. If stimulus and response elements are very different, subsequently acquired associative bonds will not effect the retention of previously acquired bonds. If stimulus elements are similar but response elements differ, subsequently acquired associative bonds will interfere with the retention of previously learned material.

For example, let us assume that you are studying the lives of American presidents, and you have just read short biographies of Ulysses S. Grant and Dwight D. Eisenhower. In these biographies you've read a number of facts. You've read that both men were graduates of West Point, that Eisenhower was once president of a university, that Grant was once a clerk in a store, and that Eisenhower reached the rank of a five-star general, whereas Grant reached the rank of a four-star general. If you read the Grant biography first and then the Eisenhower biography, the use of Associative Learning Theory would allow you to make the following predictions about what you would remember about Grant.

First, the fact that Eisenhower was a graduate of West Point would tend to <u>facilitate</u> your retention of the fact that Grant was also a graduate of West Point. Second, the fact that Eisenhower was a college president would have a <u>neutral effect</u> on your remembering that Grant was a store clerk; the positions of college president and store clerk are so different that confusion between the two is unlikely. Finally, the fact that Eisenhower was a five-star general would tend to <u>interfere</u> with your retention of the fact that Grant was a four-star general. The stimulus event—the question "What rank did so-and-so hold?"—which prompts recall of this fact is identical for either man, but the response is different in each case. This situation is likely to produce confusion as to which response is correct and thereby reduce your ability to recall the fact.

---

4. Early in the semester in a psychology class you learn that one of the principal founders of Associative Learning Theory was Edward Thorndike Later in the semester, you learn that Clark Hull contributed substantially to the subsequent development of the theory. At the end of the semester, I ask you, "Who was a principal founder of Associative Learning Theory? Will the fact that you learned about Hull facilitate, have no effect on, or interfere with your ability to remember Thorndike as the correct answer? Why?

_____

_____

_____

- - - - - - - - - - - - - - - - - -

Learning about Hull should <u>interfere</u> with your ability to remember Thorndike as the founder, because the stimulus event (the request to name a psychologist connected with Associative Learning Theory) is similar for both men, but the responses (Thorndike and Hull) are different.

5. In Chapter 1, you learned that B. F. Skinner was the principal originator of Operant Learning Theory. In the question above, you learned that Edward Thorndike was the principal originator of Associative Learning Theory. Will learning about Thorndike interfere with, have no effect on, or facilitate your ability to remember Skinner as the founder of Operant Learning Theory? Why?

_____

_____

_____

- - - - - - - - - - - - - - - - - -

It should have little effect on your ability to remember Skinner as the founder of Operant Learning Theory. You should have formed one associative bond between Skinner and Operant Learning Theory and another between Thorndike and Associative Learning Theory. The stimulus and response events are different in the two cases, and they should neither facilitate nor interfere with memory.

6. Assume you know that B. F. Skinner was a professor at an Ivy League university. Further, assume you just learned that Clark Hull had also been a professor at an Ivy League university. Would learning that Hull was an Ivy League professor facilitate, interfere with, or have no effect on your

ability to remember that Skinner was an Ivy League Professor? Why?

_____

_____

_____

- - - - - - - - - - - - - - - - -

Learning about Hull should facilitate your memory of the information about Skinner. The stimulus and the response events are similar in both cases, and learning the information about Hull should facilitate retention of the information about Skinner.

The fifth principle of Associative Learning Theory is: <u>Learning can be hierarchically organized so that lower-level skills can be chained together to serve as associative signals for the performance of higher-level skills.</u>

Thus, a complex terminal skill can be broken down into a number of subskills, and satisfactory completion of one subskill can serve as an associative signal for performing the next subskill. Subskills are "chained" together in the sequence in which they should be performed. The recitation of the alphabet represents such a "chained" subskill. Try reciting it backwards! It is difficult, because we have learned the skill so well that A automatically elicits B, B elicits C, and so on. But we have not learned the alphabet backwards, so Z does not elicit Y.

Let's take another example of this principle. Assume that your task was to teach students to find the mean (average) of a series of numbers. This terminal skill can be broken down into two subskills: computing the sum of the numbers, and dividing the sum by the number of values contributing to the sum. A hierarchy of skills for this task would look like this:

finding mean

▲

dividing sum

▲

computing sum

Completion of the computing-the-sum skill could serve as a signal that the dividing-the-sum skill should be performed, and completion of this skill results results in satisfactory terminal performance.

7. Let's return to Mr. Meyers, who teaches the automobile repair class. His problem was that Henry Fonzie could not repair a car with a mechanical problem. According to the principle above, how should Mr. Meyers approach the problem of teaching Henry this terminal skill?

_____

_ _ _ _ _ _ _ _ _ _ _ _ _ _ _ _ _

He should break the terminal skill into subskills and organize them in the sequence in which the subskills should be performed. He could then provide Henry with drill and practice on the skills and their sequence of performance. Performance of one skill should serve as a signal for performance of the next in sequence.

Before proceeding, let's review the principles governing the acquisition and retention of associative bonds.

REVIEW

8. List the five principles underlying Associative Learning Theory.

a. _____

_____

b. _____

_____

c. _____

_____

d. _____

_____

e. _____

_____

_ _ _ _ _ _ _ _ _ _ _ _ _ _ _ _ _

a. Associative bonds increase in strength as a function of repeated pairings of stimulus and response events.
b. Associative bonds decrease in strength as a function of disuse.
c. Once associative bonds have been acquired they can influence the learning of subsequent associative bonds.
d. Subsequent learning can affect the retention of previous learning.
e. Learning can be hierarchically organized so that lower-level skills can be chained together to serve as associative signals for the performance of higher-level skills.

STEPS IN APPLYING ASSOCIATIVE LEARNING THEORY
TO EDUCATIONAL PROBLEMS

Now let's discuss how Associative Learning Theory can be applied. The four steps involved in applying Associative Learning Theory to educational problems are:

1. Identify the terminal skill which is the goal of the instruction.
2. Identify the skill level the student has attained before beginning the instruction.
3. Break the terminal skill into subskills, and identify the sequence in which the subskills should be performed.
4. Design instruction so that the subskills are presented and acquired in the appropriate sequence. Make sure the instruction is presented so as to maximize the acquisition and retention of the skills.

First, identify the terminal skill which is the goal of the instruction. This step involves formulating a concise statement of the skill to be attained along with a description of how you will determine if the students have acquired the skill. You should state the terminal skills (your objectives) in behavioral terms. That is, the objectives should specify what the student will be able to do, to demonstrate that he or she has reached the terminal skill. To assess achievement of an objective stated in terms such as "the student will be able to calculate. . ." or "the student will be able to describe. . ." is much easier than to assess objectives such as "the student will appreciate. . ." or "the student will understand. . . ." If objectives are not stated in behavioral terms, it becomes very difficult to determine if the terminal skill has been satisfactorily attained. For example, you can easily assess whether a terminal skill such as "the student will be able to solve long division problems involving decimals" has been attained. However, how would you assess an objective such as "the student will be able to appreciate modern art"?

A further advantage of stating objectives in behavioral terms is that they are easily communicable. An objective such as the long division example above should be readily understood by anyone who reads it. In contrast, another person's understanding of what "to appreciate" means might be very different from yours. Close examination of the verb is a key to writing a useful behavioral objective. If the verb leads to having the student perform an observable act, then the objective is a helpful one. If the verb does not call for an observable action by the student, then the objective is not useful.

You should also specify the standard you will use to determine if an objective has been attained. Using our long-division example, the complete statement of the objective might be as follows: "The student will be able to solve long division problems involving decimals (9 of 10)." In this statement, the figures in parentheses indicate our standard: The student must solve at least nine of the ten problems correctly to show mastery of the objective. As the teacher, you would choose whatever standard (for example, 4 of 5, 7 of 8, 4 of 4) you feel is appropriate for your students and your subject matter.

=====

9. Assume you were teaching a class in natural history, and you wanted to teach students to correctly identify ten different minerals. How would you state your objective?

_____

_____

_____

- - - - - - - - - - - - - - - - - -

Your objective should be similar to the following one: "The student should be able to correctly identify and label minerals (9 of 10)."

=====

The second step in applying Associative Learning Theory is to identify the skill level the student has attained before beginning the instruction. The purpose of this step is to determine the level at which a task analysis (the next step) should begin. Ideally, this step should occur at the beginning of a school year. The best technique for identifying skill level involves constructing a pretest which assesses skills both above and below the student's expected skill level. For example, if you want to start the year by teaching students to solve whole-number division problems, you might develop a test which assessed multiplication and subtraction skills (lower-level skills which should have already been mastered), whole-number division skills (skills at the target level), and division of decimals (skills above the target level). The results of this test could then be used to identify the level at which task analysis should begin. For instance, if the results indicate that the student has not mastered multiplication skills, then the task analysis should begin at this level. Likewise, if the results indicate that a student has mastered all of the skills assessed on the test, then a task analysis should begin at a higher-level skill than had been included on the test. (You might want to give another test to see if the student has mastered skills on an even higher level.) This testing procedure assures that instruction begins at a level consonant with the student's development. Slower students will not be presented with instruction they are unprepared to handle, and brighter students will not have to repeat instruction they have already mastered.

The third step in applying Associative Learning Theory to educational problems is to break the terminal skill (identified in the second step) into subskills, and identify the sequence in which the subskills should be performed. Let's look first at the breakdown of skills. This breakdown, often known as task analysis, is important for two reasons.

First, analysis of a complex terminal skill into its component subskills makes explicit the skills which must be taught. For example, analysis of the subskills involved in finding a mean shows that we must teach two subskills in a given sequence before the terminal skill can be attained.

Second, task analysis is important because it provides a means for determining where instruction has failed. For example, assume that performance of a terminal skill involves performing four subskills in a particular order. Let's say that at the end of instruction, the students can't perform the terminal skill. The teacher could then look at performance on the subskills to determine the <u>specific</u> <u>point</u> at which the instruction failed. Using our example of finding the mean, students may be able to add perfectly well but may have trouble with division. As a result, they can't find the mean. This indicates that the instructional sequence involving division would have to be revised until the student could successfully perform this subskill.

One question you might have concerning task analysis is, "How deep do I go in identifying subskills?" Obviously, even simple skills such as finding a mean can be analyzed far more deeply than we have analyzed them. We could identify component skills in both addition and division, and we could probably identify even more basic skills making up these component skills. The answer to this question is that you stop analyzing skills into their component parts at the level indicated by your entering pretest (see the previous step). If a student can satisfactorily perform a particular complex skill, you may safely assume that all of the lower-level skills have been mastered.

The second part of a task analysis is to determine <u>the</u> <u>sequence</u> <u>in</u> <u>which</u> <u>the</u> <u>subskills</u> <u>must</u> <u>be</u> <u>performed</u> <u>in</u> <u>order</u> <u>to</u> <u>perform</u> <u>the</u> <u>terminal</u> <u>skill.</u> A student must master a sequence in which component subskills must be performed, as well as the skills themselves, in order to attain mastery of the terminal skill. This step is important, since students might possess all of the necessary skills but still be unable to perform the terminal skill, because they were not sure of the order in which the skills should be performed.

---

10. Suppose you are a teacher who wants to teach your students how to use a dictionary to look up words they do not understand. First, write an objective for this terminal skill.

_____

_____

_____

Second, perform a task analysis on the skill. That is, list the subskills in the sequence in which they must be performed in order to perform the terminal skill.

_____

_____

_____

- - - - - - - - - - - - - - - - - - -

Your objective should be similar to the following one: The student should be able to use a dictionary to find the correct definition of unfamiliar words (10 of 10).

Your task analysis should include the following steps (1) Look at the initial letter of the unfamiliar word and turn to the section of the dictionary containing words beginning with that letter; (2) look at the second letter of the word and turn to the section of the dictionary containing words which begin with the first and second letters of the word; (3) continue the process of looking at successive letters of the word until the word is found in the dictionary; and (4) write down the definition of the unfamiliar word.

REVIEW

11. Answer the following questions:

a. Who was the principal founder of Associative Learning Theory?

_____

b. Who was the principal founder of applied Operant Learning Theory?

_____

c. Where was B. F. Skinner a professor?

_____

- - - - - - - - - - - - - - - - - - -

Return to answers 4, 5, and 6, to see if our predictions about your ability to answer these questions were borne out. (If you are taking a course, check with your fellow students so you can look at data from more than one person).

The fourth, and final step, in applying Associative Learning Theory to an educational problem is to design instruction so that the subskills are presented and acquired in the appropriate sequence, in a way that will maximize the acquisition and retention of the skills. The first part of this step is straightforward. The instruction should be designed to attain the objective established in the first step in the process of applying Associative Learning Theory to an educational problem. Instruction should begin at the level identified by the pretest in our second step and should systematically cover the subskills in their appropriate sequence as identified by the third step.

To maximize acquisition and retention of the skills, we will design the instruction in accordance with the principles of Associative Learning Theory. Guidelines for designing the instruction in this manner are presented below.

Sufficient practice should be provided on the new skills to assure that they are well learned. This guideline is in accordance with the first principle of Associative Learning Theory which says that repeated practice on stimulus and response events strengthens the associative bonds between those events.

Frequent review of each newly acquired skill should be provided to maintain that skill at a high level. This guideline is in accordance with the second principle of Associative Learning Theory which says that the strength of associative bonds decreases with disuse. Frequent practice can maintain previously acquired skills at a high level of strength.

The instructional material should be prepared to facilitate learning and minimize interference. This guideline is in accordance with the third and fourth principles of Associative Learning Theory which say that previously acquired associative bonds can influence subsequently acquired bonds, and that subsequently acquired bonds can influence the retention of previously learned material. The positive educational effects of these principles can be maximized in two ways. First, when new material is similar to previously learned material (both stimulus and response elements), the similarities should be emphasized to facilitate learning of the new material and to minimize forgetting of the previously learned material. Second, when the materials involve the learning of different responses to similar stimulus events, the stimulus events should be carefully distinguished to minimize interference in acquiring the new material and retaining the old material.

The instruction should be presented so that the skills first acquired form the foundation for learning subsequent higher-order skills. This guideline is in accordance with the fifth principle of Associative Learning Theory which says that learning should occur in sequence so that lower-level skills can serve as signals for the performance of higher-level skills. This guideline can be fulfilled by presenting subskills in the sequence identified previously in the process of applying Associative Learning Theory to an educational problem.

Practice in applying these guidelines to a simulated educational problem will be provided in the next chapter. Let's review the steps involved in applying Associative Learning Theory to an educational problem.

REVIEW

12. List the four steps involved in applying Associative Learning Theory to an educational problem.

a. _____

b. _____

c. _____

d. _____

_____

_____

- - - - - - - - - - - - - - - - - -

a. Identify the terminal skill which is the goal of the instruction.
b. Identify the skill level the student has attained before beginning the instruction.
c. Break the terminal skill into subskills, and identify the sequence in which the subskills should be performed.
d. Design instruction so that the subskills are presented and acquired in the appropriate sequence. This design should incorporate features which maximize the acquisition and retention of the skills.

SUMMARY

In this chapter we have reviewed the basics of applying Associative Learning Theory to an educational problem. We have described the type of situation where Associative Learning Theory might be profitably used, and have discussed the five basic principles underlying Associative Learning Theory. We have also discussed four steps for applying the theory. Chapter 4 will provide you with practice in working through each of these steps.

ADDITIONAL READINGS

Anderson, J. R., and Bower, G. H. Human Associative Memory. Washington D.C.: V. H. Winston & Sons, 1973.

Deese, J., and Hulse, S. H. The Psychology of Learning (3rd ed.). New York McGraw-Hill, 1967.

Dixon, T. R., and Horton, D. L. Verbal Behavior and General Behavior Theory. Englewood Cliffs, New Jersey: Prentice-Hall, 1968.

Gagné, R. M. The Conditions of Learning (2nd ed.). New York: Holt, Rinehar & Winston, 1970.

Hall, J. F. The Psychology of Learning. Philadelphia: J. B. Lippincott, 1966

SELF-TEST

This self-test is designed to show you whether or not you have mastered the objectives of Chapter 3. Answer each question to the best of your ability, based on what you learned in this chapter. Correct answers are given following the test.

1. For what type of educational situation or problem would Associative Learning Theory be most useful?

    _____

    _____

    _____

2. What is the basic assumption underlying Associative Learning Theory?

    _____

    _____

    _____

3. List the five basic principles underlying Associative Learning Theory.

    a. _____

    _____

    b. _____

    _____

    c. _____

    _____

    d. _____

    _____

    e. _____

    _____

4. List the four steps required to implement an Associative Learning Theory program.

    a. _____

    _____

b. _____
   _____

c. _____
   _____

d. _____
   _____

ANSWERS TO SELF-TEST

Compare your answers to the questions on the self-test with the answers given below. If all of your answers are correct, you are ready to go on to the next chapter. If you missed any questions, review the appropriate parts of the chapter before you go on.

1. Associative Learning Theory is most useful in situations where a lack of critical basic skills is preventing a student from benefiting from instruction.

2. The basic assumption underlying Associative Learning Theory is that learning involves a process of forming "associative bonds" between stimulus events and response events.

3. The five basic principles underlying Associative Learning Theory are:

    a. Associative bonds increase in strength as a function of repeated pairings of stimulus and response events.
    b. Associative bonds decrease in strength as a function of disuse.
    c. Once associative bonds have been acquired, they can influence the learning of subsequent associative bonds.
    d. Subsequent learning can affect the retention of prior learning.
    e. Learning can be hierarchically organized so that lower-level skills can be chained together to serve as associative units for the performance of higher-level skills.

4. The four steps required to implement an Associative Learning Theory program are:

    a. Identify the terminal skill which is the goal of the instruction.
    b. Identify the skill level the student has attained before beginning the instruction.
    c. Break the terminal skill into subskills, and identify the sequence in which the subskills should be performed.
    d. Design instruction so that the subskills are presented and acquired in the appropriate sequence. Make sure the instruction is presented so as to maximize the acquisition and retention of the skills.

CHAPTER FOUR
Application of Associative
Learning Theory
to Educational Problems

Chapter 4 will give you some practice in applying Associative Learning Theory to an educational problem. After completing this chapter you should be able to:

1. Analyze an educational problem situation to determine if the use of Associative Learning Theory is appropriate.
2. Use the steps from Associative Learning Theory to develop instructional materials.
3. Review an instructional sequence to insure that the principles of Associative Learning Theory are reflected in the instruction.

IDENTIFYING SITUATIONS
WHERE ASSOCIATIVE LEARNING THEORY IS APPROPRIATE

In Chapter 3, we indicated that Associative Learning Theory would be most appropriately applied in situations where the educational problem involves the absence of critical basic skills. We noted that you must be able to define clearly and to measure objectively the terminal skill or goal of the instruction as well as the subskills which contribute to performance of the terminal skill.

One other characteristic must be present in a situation before Associative Learning Theory can be used successfully: The students must be attentive and motivated to learn. The best set of learning materials in the world would be wasted if the students paid no attention to the materials.

1. If faced with a situation where students are inattentive and unmotivated, and you have tried virtually everything but nothing seems to work, what would you do?

_____

_____

We would try applied Operant Learning Theory.

Now let's look at several situations and decide if Associative Learning Theory is suitable.

2. Mary Hecht is a very good student in your high school biology class, and she has approached you with a problem. She wants to prepare a project consisting of a highly original experiment for an upcoming national science contest. Her idea is to conduct an experiment which will demonstrate that the territorial behavior of certain tropical fish is triggered by competition for scarce food supplies and sexual partners. She wants you to help her develop the skills necessary for designing and conducting a project which would have a good chance of winning the competition. Is this a problem where Associative Learning Theory would be useful? Why, or why not?

_____

_____

_____

- - - - - - - - - - - - - - - - - -

No, some of the elements which would allow Associative Learning Theory to be used are missing in this situation. The problem is appropriate, because it involves a lack of critical skills. But neither the desired skill (designing a highly original experiment) nor the subskills making up the terminal skill are clearly defined, nor is there an objective way to measure them. The ability to conceive and carry out a highly original experiment moves into the poorly understood area of creativity. We can help Mary learn about tropical fish, but we cannot give her a handy procedure for coming up with a prize-winning project.

3. Clifford Bates is a student enrolled in a freshman English course. He is having a great deal of difficulty in writing essays for the course. His mechanics (spelling, punctuation, grammar, and the like) are adequate, but he seems to write without purpose. His essays ramble on, and the reader finds it very difficult to determine what Clifford is trying to say. Is this a problem which could be approached by using Associative Learning Theory? Why, or why not?

_____

_____

_____

- - - - - - - - - - - - - - - - - -

Yes, it is. First, the problem involves the basic skill of being able to write in an organized, purposeful fashion. Second, the terminal skill can be objectively measured by examining a writing sample to determine if the key elements of purposeful writing are contained in the sample. And, third, the elements making up the terminal essay-writing skill (for example, initial statement of thesis, development of arguments contained in thesis, restatement of thesis in light of discussion of arguments) can be isolated, defined, and objectively measured.

4.   Greg Wallin is a fifth grader who is always chosen last in the class softball games played at recess. Greg has become very self-conscious about being chosen last, and he sometimes pretends he is ill to avoid going out to recess. Is this a problem which could be approached by applying Associative Learning Theory? Why, or why not?

_____

_____

_____

- - - - - - - - - - - - - - - - -

This problem is interesting in that it involves two parts, each of which would invite the application of a different learning theory. The first problem is social in nature. The fact that Greg's classmates always choose him last has contributed to his lack of self-confidence. This part of the problem could be helped by using applied Operant Learning Theory to encourage Greg's classmates to make him feel he is a more valued participant in the softball games.

   The second part of the problem involves Greg's lack of athletic skills. This problem could be approached by using Associative Learning Theory to increase Greg's athletic competence. Any well-performed athletic skill involves mastery of a series of subskills which contribute to performance of the terminal skill. Softball can be broken down into skills such as throwing, batting, fielding, and strategy. These skills can, in turn, be broken into even finer skills. Associative Learning Theory could be applied to analyze the complex skill of playing softball, and to develop systematic instruction in the basic physical skills which would lead to improvement in Greg's ability to play softball.

APPLYING THE STEPS IN ASSOCIATIVE LEARNING THEORY TO AN EDUCATIONAL PROBLEM

In this section we will present you with a case study and systematically work through each of the steps in applying Associative Learning Theory to an educational problem. First, let's review the steps. If you'd like to check your memory, write out the four steps. Otherwise, just review the steps below and go on to the case study.

REVIEW

5. What are the four steps to follow when applying Associative Learning Theory to an educational problem?

1. _____

_____

2. _____

_____

3. _____

_____

4. _____

_____

- - - - - - - - - - - - - - - - - - - -

1. Identify the terminal skill (instructional objective) which is the goal of the instruction.
2. Identify the skill level the student has attained before beginning the instruction.
3. Break the terminal skill into subskills, and identify the sequence in which the subskills should be performed.
4. Design instruction so that the subskills are presented and acquired in the appropriate sequence. This design should incorporate features which maximize the acquisition and retention of the skills.

Case Study. You are teaching a course on home management and business practices at the high school level. As part of your course, you teach students how to balance a checkbook. On the past two final examinations, your students did very poorly in this area. Until now, your approach to teaching checkbook balancing has been rather relaxed. However, because of the poor performance on the exams, you are now concerned that students are leaving your class without having mastered this important skill. After considering this situation, you decide that Associative Learning Theory provides a suitable approach to your problem.

The first step in applying Associative Learning Theory to this problem involves identifying the terminal skill which is the goal of the instruction—that is, formulating an instructional objective for the skill you want your students to master.

6. Given the information in the case study, write an instructional objective for the problem. (If you wish to review the elements which should be contained in an instructional objective, refer back to pages 81-82 in Chapter 3.)

_____

_____

_____

_____

- - - - - - - - - - - - - - - - - -

Your objective should contain a concise statement of the skills to be acquired, as well as a description of the method you will use to determine if the students have acquired the skills. Our sample objective is: Given give sample checkbooks and five bank statements (some of which include common errors), the students will be able to correct the errors and balance all five checkbooks.

Now we are ready for the second step: to identify the skill level the students have attained before beginning instruction. The purpose of this step is to identify the place where our task analysis should begin. That is, we want to be able to locate the place in a skill hierarchy where all of the skills below the identified point have been mastered, and all of the skills above the identified point have not been mastered. Our task analysis can then focus on the unmastered skills.

Completion of this step involves several stages. The first stage is to identify the lower-level skills which must be mastered before a student can successfully perform the terminal skill of balancing a checkbook.

7. List all of the skills that must be mastered before a person can successfully balance a checkbook. Start your list with simple arithmetic skills.

_____

_____

_____

_____

- - - - - - - - - - - - - - - - - -

Your list should contain the following subskills (though it need not be identical to our list).

1. Perform addition involving decimals.
2. Perform subtraction involving decimals.
3. Be able to identify all of the information contained on a bank statement.
4. Be able to correctly balance a sample checkbook when given the checkbook and a bank statement.

The items we have listed in Answer 7 can serve as the basis for generating a pretest which will assess the entering skill levels of the students. Items 1, 2, and 3 in our list are all preskills, which must be mastered before a student can perform the terminal skill of balancing a checkbook. We have also included (Item 4) the actual terminal skill.

---

8. Why do you think we included the terminal skill in our list? That is, why would measuring the terminal skill be useful in an instrument designed to assess the entering skill level of students?

_____

_____

_____

- - - - - - - - - - - - - - - - - -

Some of the students may have mastered the checkbook-balancing skill before instruction begins. If so, measuring the terminal skill in our entering test will allow us to identify those students, and we can avoid wasting their time with instruction they do not need. We also noted in Chapter 3 that it is a good idea to include skills on your pretest which are more advanced than your target skill. You can then identify students who are well ahead of their classmates.

Having identified the skills which should be assessed in our entering level test, we are now ready to construct and administer a pretest designed to determine whether the identified skills have been mastered. Imagine that we constructed a pretest which contained (1) five addition problems involving decimals, (2) five subtraction problems containing decimals, (3) five bank statements on which the students had to identify the checks cashed column, the deposits column, and the balance column, and (4) two sample checkbooks and bank statements that the students were asked to balance.

Assume that we administered this pretest to a group of ten students. The test results for the ten students are presented in Table 1.

Table 1. Percentage of Correct Problems on Each of the Four Skills

Student	Addition	Subtraction	Identification	Checkbook Balancing
Bill	100	100	100	0
Mary	100	100	100	0
Sally	100	100	100	50
Tom	100	100	100	100
Harry	100	100	60	0
Susan	100	100	100	0
Pat	100	40	0	0
Sarah	100	100	100	100
Mike	100	100	100	0
Tim	100	100	100	0

8. After examining the data in Table 1, determine where instruction should begin for each of the ten students:

Bill: _____

Mary: _____

Sally: _____

Tom: _____

Harry: _____

Susan: _____

Pat: _____

Sarah: _____

Mike: _____

Tim: _____

- - - - - - - - - - - - - - - - - - -

Bill: Mastered first three skills. Needs instruction on checkbook balancing.

Mary: Mastered first three skills. Needs instruction on checkbook balancing.

Sally: Mastered first three skills. Balanced one checkbook correctly but made error on the second. Needs at least some instruction on chec book balancing.

Tom: Mastered all four skills. Does not need instruction on checkbook balancing.

Harry: Mastered first two skills. Correctly identified items on three bank statements but made errors on remaining two. Needs instruction on both bank statement identification and on checkbook balancing.

Susan: Mastered first three skills. Needs instruction on checkbook balancing.

Pat: Mastered first skill and shows some knowledge of second. Needs instruction on subtraction, bank statement identification, and checkbook balancing.

Sarah: Mastered all four skills. Needs no further instruction on checkbook balancing.

Mike: Mastered first three skills. Needs instruction on checkbook balancing.

Tim: Mastered first three skills. Needs instruction on checkbook balancing.

We now know that two of our ten students have already mastered our terminal skill and need no further instruction in this area. In an actual classroom setting, these students could proceed on to the next skill to be acquired in the class, or they could work on individual learning projects while the rest of the class was acquiring the checkbook-balancing skill.

We also know that six of the remaining eight students have mastered the three preskills we identified and are ready to begin instruction which will lead to mastery of the checkbook-balancing skill. The remaining two students have demonstrated deficiencies in the mastery of necessary preskills. Harry should be given remedial instruction which will lead to mastery of the identification preskill, and Pat should receive remedial instruction on both the subtraction preskill and the identification preskill.

Having completed our assessment of entering skills level, we are now ready to go on to the third step in applying Associative Learning Theory. The third step is to break the terminal skill into subskills, and identify the sequence in which the subskills should be performed—that is, to perform a task analysis. Since most of the students have mastered the three necessary preskills but not the terminal skill, we will confine our example to a task analysis of the checkbook-balancing skill (the terminal skill).

---

9. Since all of you reading this text can (we hope!) balance your own checkbooks, try performing a task analysis on this skill. Your analysis should identify each of the steps you have to go through after receiving your bank statement to successfully balance your checkbook. List these steps below. (For the moment, don't worry about the sequence of the steps.)

_____

_____

_____

_____

_____

_____

- - - - - - - - - - - - - - - - - -

Your analysis should contain the following steps:

1. List all checks recorded in the checkbook which have not been returned with the bank statement. Total these checks and subtract the total from the current balance listed on the bank statement. The resulting amount should agree with the last balance entered in the checkbook.
2. Sort the cancelled checks contained with the bank statement into numeri cal order or into order of the dates issued.
3. In the checkbook, check off each cancelled check opposite its number or date. Also make sure that the amount on the cancelled check agrees with the amount recorded in the checkbook.
4. Subtract from the checkbook balance the service charge appearing on the bank statement.

We have now completed the first part of our task analysis and are ready to proceed to the second part, which is to identify the sequence in which each of the subskills must be performed in order to correctly perform the terminal skill.

10. Refer back to Answer 9. Arrange each of the subskills in Answer 9 in the sequence in which they must be performed while balancing a checkbook.

_____

_____

_____

_____

_____

_____

- - - - - - - - - - - - - - - - - -

Your sequence should be:

1. Sort the cancelled checks contained with the bank statement into numeri cal order or into order of the dates issued.
2. In the checkbook, check off each cancelled check opposite its number or date. Also make sure that the amount on the cancelled check agrees with the amount recorded in the checkbook.

3. Subtract from the checkbook balance the service charge appearing on the bank statement.
4. List all checks recorded in the checkbook which have not been returned with the bank statement. Total these checks and subtract the total from the current balance listed on the bank statement. The resulting amount should agree with the last balance entered in the checkbook.

Now we are ready to design some instructional materials, which is the fourth step in applying Associative Learning Theory to an educational problem. The instruction should be designed so that the subskills are presented and acquired in the appropriate sequence, following the principles of Associative Learning Theory to maximize the acquisition and retention of the skills.

REVIEW

11. List the five principles of Associative Learning Theory.

1. _____
_____

2. _____
_____

3. _____
_____

4. _____
_____

5. _____
_____

- - - - - - - - - - - - - - - - - - - -

1. Associative bonds increase in strength as a function of repeated pairings of stimulus and response events.
2. Associative bonds decrease in strength as a function of disuse.
3. Once associative bonds have been acquired, they can influence the learning of subsequent associative bonds. This influence can be positive (making new learning easier), neutral (having no effect on new learning), or negative (making new learning harder).
4. Subsequent learning can affect the retention of previous learning. This influence can be positive (helping retention), neutral (having no effect on retention), or negative (hindering retention).

5. Learning can be hierarchically organized so that lower-level skills can be chained together to serve as associative signals for the perform ance of higher-level skills.

Instructional materials should be designed to maximize positive learning and retention. For example, considerable practice should be provided on each of the skills to be acquired (Principle 1), and frequent review should be given to assure that the skills are not lost through disuse (Principle 2). We must take care to point out explicitly similarities between new skills to be learned and old skills already acquired (Principles 3 and 4). In doing so, two positive events occur. First, the retention of previously learned skills is enhanced as a function of emphasizing their relationship to the skills to be acquired. Second, the acquisition of the new skills will be facilitated since the student can transfer the old skills to the new learning situation. Also, different responses to similar stimuli should be carefully distinguised to minimize interference (Principles 3 and 4).

12. Now, try your hand at designing an instructional sequence. You should spend some time on this exercise. You should approach this task in the following way. First, carefully examine the set of subskills we have identified (see Answer 10). Then design a set of exercises or instructiona experiences which will lead to mastery of each of the skills. Assume that instructional materials are readily available, and, when designing your exercises or experiences, keep the principles of Associative Learning Theory in mind. Your instructional sequence should be designed to maxi-mize the learning and retention of the skills. Ready? Describe an instruc-tional sequence to teach checkbook balancing.

_____

_____

_____

_____

_____

_____

_____

_____

_____

_____

_____

- - - - - - - - - - - - - - - - - -

Many acceptable ways of designing an instructional sequence exist. Our instructional sequence is presented below.

Step 1: Pass out sample packets of bank statements, checkbooks, and cancelled checks to the class. The cancelled checks in the packet should contain a variety of problems such as (1) some of the checks in a given packet are numbered and some are not; (2) several of the checks are misdated; (3) several of the checks are written for amounts different from those recorded in the checkbook; and (4) several of the checks were written on the same date.

   After the packets have been passed out, ask the students to sort the checks in order by date, number, or both. When the cancelled checks are sorted correctly, ask the students to mix them up and exchange packets. After giving a number of practice exercises in check sorting, proceed to the second step of instruction.

Step 2: Have the students sort a new packet of checks. Then have them check off each cancelled check in the checkbook opposite its number or date. In addition, have them check to see if the amount of each cancelled check agrees with the amount listed in the checkbook. If it does not, ask them to correct the amount listed in the checkbook and revise the checkbook balance.

   After the students have correctly completed their packets, have them exchange packets and practice with a new packet. After several practices, proceed to the third step.

Step 3: Identify for the students the place on the bank statement where the service charge appears and explain that this charge should be subtracted from the balance listed in the checkbook. Have the students practice this step a number of times with different packets. Go on to the fourth step.

Step 4: Have the students list all of the checks recorded in the checkbook which were not returned with the bank statement. Then have them total these checks and subtract this total from the balance listed in the bank statement. The final step involves comparing the resultant total with the balance listed in the checkbook. The two figures should agree. Have the students exchange packets and go through the steps several times until the skills are well practiced.

The instructional sequence we present in Answer 12 contains a number of elements which should also be included in your own sequence. Instruction is presented in the appropriate order, and considerable practice is provided on each of the skills to assure that they are well learned. If we were using this sequence in an actual classroom situation, we would also provide periodic review of the terminal skill to assure that the students would not lose it through disuse.

In an actual classroom situation, several additional strategies could be used to maximize the learning and retention of the instructional materials. For example, in a course on home management and business practices, students would learn a number of highly similar skills. For example, home budgeting, home accounting, tax report preparation, and checkbook balancing all involve the repeated usage of a common set of basic skills, such as addition, subtraction, and listing procedures. The teacher could make new material easier to learn and maximize retention by explicitly pointing out that the basic skills used in a previously learned activity are the same as those involved in the current activity.

While a situation which involves the repeated usage of a common set of basic skills for different learning activities provides many opportunities to faciliate transfer of learning, it also negatively affects learning and retention. For example, even though tax preparation, checkbook balancing, home budgeting, and home accounting share several common basic skills, all of the skills in these activities are not the same. Further, the sequence in which the skills are used is likely to be different in each of the activities. This situation provides a setting where students could easily confuse the set of skills and the sequence in which they are performed for one activity with those from another activity.

To guard against this happening, a teacher must devise a way of differentiating the set of skills employed in one activity from those employed in a different activity. One very effective way of doing this is to use a memory device called a mnemonic. A mnemonic is a sentence, a word, or even a rhyme which helps us remember things. For example, many of us use the rhyme "i before e except after c" to help us spell words correctly. Another example is the familiar "thirty days hath September, April, June, and November." A mnemonic can be used in situations like the one we have described to differentiate between the activities involved in the performance of skills sharing common elements. For instance, our checkbook balancing skills involved performing the following activities.

1. Sort the cancelled checks.
2. Check off each cancelled check in the checkbook.
3. Subtract service charge.

4. <u>List</u> nonreturned checks, <u>total</u> them, and subtract the total from the balance shown in the bank statement.

Given this list of activities, we can make up a mnemonic which encodes the particular skills and the sequence in which they are to be performed. For example, our mnemonic might be: "To balance a checkbook, sorted checks subtract from the listed total. " We can then have the students memorize this sentence; if they can recall the sentence, they can decode the skills and the sequence in which they are to be performed.

If we make up a different mnemonic for each of the terminal skills we wish to teach (checkbook balancing, home accounting, and the like), we will have provided the students with a way of differentiating between the activities involved in the various terminal skills. The result should be a reduction in the amount of negative transfer which will occur.

EVALUATING THE EFFECTIVENESS OF YOUR INSTRUCTION

In this chapter we have given you some practice in recognizing the type of situation where Associative Learning Theory might be appropriately applied, and we have systematically worked through an example following each of the steps for developing an instructional sequence based on Associative Learning Theory. One step remains: You must evaluate the effectiveness of your instruction.

The method of evaluation is described in the instructional objective written in the first step of the process of applying Associative Learning Theory to an educational problem. For example, in our case study, the goal of instruction was: Given five sample checkbooks and bank statements (some of which contain common errors), the students will be able to correct the errors and balance all five checkbooks. We would evaluate the effectiveness of our instruction by presenting the students with the five checkbooks and bank statements to see if they can correctly perform the task. If the students can balance all five checkbooks, we know that our instruction has been effective. If the students cannot balance all five checkbooks, we know that we have to revise our instructional procedures.

In a situation where the students did not reach the instructional objective, the task and sequence analysis completed in step 3 of the process of applying Associative Learning Theory is a useful tool for locating the point at which instruction failed. For example, let's imagine that we closely examine the work of students who could not correctly balance their checkbooks. We notice that all of these students have correctly sorted the checks, so the instruction on Subskill 1 is sufficient. They have checked to see that the amount on each cancelled check agrees with the amount listed in the checkbook (Subskill 2 instruction is clear). However, at this point in the sequence, things go awry. After completing the check-off activity, some of the students begin to total the checks, some begin to subtract checks from the bank statement balance, and some do nothing more. This pattern of activity suggests that our instruction is weak in the sequence transition between Subskills 3 and 4. Therefore, we would revise our instruction to place greater emphasis on this activity.

The cycle of setting instructional goals, designing instruction to fulfill those goals, checking to see if students have met the goals, and revising instruction if the goals are not met is an extraordinarily powerful tool for developing instructional procedures which work. One is always striving for 100 percent success. A teacher can strive for no higher goal!

ADDITIONAL READINGS

Allan, R. G. Writing Behavioral Objectives and Criterion Tests. Holyoke, Massachusetts: Scott Educational Division, 1972.

Anderson, R. C., and Faust, G. W. Educational Psychology: The Science of Instruction. New York: Dodd, Mead, 1973.

Gagné, R. M. Essentials of Learning for Instruction. Hillsdale, Illinois: Dryden Press, 1974.

Kolesnik, W. B. Learning: Educational Applications. Boston: Allyn and Bacon, 1976.

Mager, R. F. Preparing Instructional Objectives. Palo Alto, California: Fearon Publishers, 1962.

Mager, R. G. Goal Analysis. Belmont, California: Fearon Publishers, 1972.

Snelbecker, G. F. Learning Theory, Instructional Theory, and Psychoeducational Design. New York: McGraw-Hill, 1974.

SELF-TEST

This self-test is designed to show you whether or not you have mastered the
objectives of Chapter 4. Answer each question to the best of your ability,
based on what you learned in this chapter. Correct answers are given following the test.

1. Mr. Jones is a geography teacher. He has found that students are having
    difficulty analyzing geographical problems. Further probing has shown
    the problem to be a lack of basic understanding of geographical concepts.
    What learning theory should Mr. Jones employ?

    _____   a. Operant Learning Theory
    _____   b. Associative Learning Theory
    _____   c. Cognitive Learning Theory

2. Imagine you are teaching a class. Select a problem and try to work through
    each of the five steps required to implement Associative Learning Theory
    in your own classroom. (No one correct answer can be given, since you
    are selecting the problem, but the answers will allow you to evaluate your
    approach.)

    a. Specify the terminal skill.

    _____

    _____

    b. Before you begin instruction, how will you determine the skill level
       the students have already attained?

    _____

    _____

    _____

    c. Break your terminal skill into its component subskills and sequence
       the subskills.

    _____

    _____

    _____

    d. Prepare an instructional approach which uses the principles of Associa-
       tive Learning Theory. Describe in detail the steps in your lesson, how
       you will organize your students, what instruction materials you will use,
       and how you will insure that all students have mastered all subskills lead-
       ing to your terminal skill. Be sure to incorporate the principles of
       Associative Learning Theory into your instructional approach.

ANSWERS TO SELF-TEST

Compare your answers to the questions on the self-test with the answers given below. If all of your answers are correct, you are ready to go on to the next chapter. If you missed any questions, review the appropriate parts of the chapter before you go on.

1. Associative Learning Theory

2. Since you are working with a situation you selected, no "correct" answer can be given. However, we have listed ideas that you should have considered for each step.

   a. Is the terminal skill a major goal of your course? Is it an activity that has a meaning by itself—for instance, writing a letter, conducting a scientific experiment, or analyzing a political problem? Is the statement written so that the verb indicates an activity that can be observed? Do you state how well the skill must be performed?

   b. You must pretest. List previous skills that lead to your terminal skill. Prepare a test based on those previous skills. When you test your students, you will discover what you must teach and what each student in the class already knows. This information is important for preparing your instruction and for properly grouping your students.

   c. When you broke your terminal skill into its components, did you list them as observable behaviors? Each of these subskills must be a behavior that can be observed and measured. How are the subskills sequenced? You do have a number of options (for example, simple to difficult, known to unknown, in the order they will be performed when performing the terminal skill). If in doubt, the simple-to-difficult sequence is probably your best bet.

   d. Did you list each of the subskills and group students so they begin at the appropriate spot in the sequence? You must have a list or measurement device to insure mastery of each subskill before the student proceeds to the next one. Finally, your lessons (for example, presentations, assignments, work sheets) should be organized so that the principles of Associative Learning are built into the approach. These principles include:

      —Repetition
      —Practice of subskills later in the process if necessary
      —Using associative bonds learned earlier to help with later learning
      —Taking care not to let confusion occur when similar stimuli are connected to different responses
      —Organizing the learning in a hierarchy from lower level skills to more complex skills

This question has been rather long and complex to work through. If you have had any difficulty with any of the four steps, you may wish to reread the chapter or discuss the problem with an experienced teacher for additional help in thinking through an issue such as breaking a complex skill into subskills, grouping students, or building retention into lessons.

PART THREE
Cognitive Learning Theory

CHAPTER FIVE
Principles of Cognitive Learning Theory for Classroom Use

Cognitive Learning Theory is the newest of the theories we will present in this book. A number of psychologists, including Edward Tolman and Sir Frederick Bartlett, who were working in the 1930s and 1940s, could be considered early cognitive psychologists. However, not until the mid-1960s did Cognitive Learning Theory become a major theory in psychology. One event which contributed greatly to the emergence of cognitive psychology as a major force was the increased understanding and use of computers in the social sciences. During the 1960s some psychologists began to ask if the way in which computers process, store, and retrieve information could be analogous to the way in which human beings perform the same activities. This and similar questions stimulated the development of a theory which is quite different than the theories we have considered so far.

In this chapter we will examine Cognitive Learning Theory, noting how the assumptions underlying the theory are quite different from those underlying applied Operant Learning Theory and Associative Learning Theory. Then we will discuss the kind of educational situation to which Cognitive Learning Theory might be applied and the basic principles involved. The final section will present some of the techniques which have proven to be useful when applying the theory in instructional settings.

After completing this chapter, you should be able to:

1. List and explain the elements of Cognitive Learning Theory.
2. Describe how the assumptions underlying Cognitive Learning Theory differ from those underlying Associative Learning Theory and applied Operant Learning Theory.
3. Describe the kinds of educational situation where Cognitive Learning Theory might be applied.
4. List the basic principles involved in applying Cognitive Learning Theory to an educational problem.
5. Describe the techniques for applying Cognitive Learning Theory to an educational problem.

A MODEL OF COGNITIVE LEARNING THEORY

Cognitive Learning Theory was developed with the intention of describing how human beings process, store, and retrieve information. Perhaps the simplest way to give you an overview of Cognitive Learning Theory is to present a simplified model of human information processing:

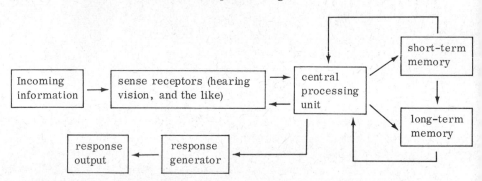

Before considering how information moves through this model, we will briefly describe each component.

Incoming information is any kind of information we can perceive in our environment. Sounds, sights, odors, and tactile sensations are all examples of incoming information.

Sense receptors are the organs which perceive the incoming information. The receptors correspond to the familiar senses of hearing, seeing, smelling, tasting, and touching.

The central processing unit is the "manager" of the entire information-processing system. The central processing unit decides what information is worthy of complete processing and what is not. It decides where incoming information should be stored and directs the retrieval and output of information being recalled.

Short-term memory is a limited-capacity storage area which stores incoming information for a brief period of time. Information which is not subjected to further processing decays from short-term memory after about fifteen seconds.

Long-term memory is a storage area thought to have an unlimited capacity and an unlimited duration. That is, the amount of information that can be stored in long-term memory appears to be unlimited, and, once stored, that information is permanent. Information in long-term memory is stored in an organized, structured fashion. For example, one way in which the structure of long-term memory has been conceptualized is as a knowledge hierarchy. As an example, part of a hypothetical hierarchy depicting our knowledge about animals is presented on the following page.

Cognitive Learning Theory suggests that such knowledge structures are established as a child develops. During development, children add new information to the structures and on occasion reformulate major structures. For

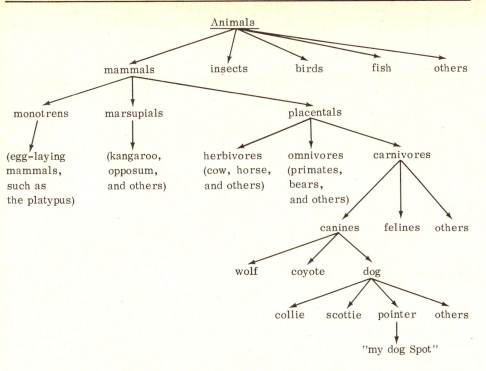

example, not surprisingly, a young child may have completely separate structures for information about mammals and about insects. As the child develops
and gains more information about the world around, he or she might reformulate the two separate structures into a single structure incorporating information about both types of animals.

Response generators are the systems that allow us to respond and com-
municate. Our vocal and motor systems are examples of response generators.

Response output is the output from a response generator. It could be a
spoken word, a movement, or even a thought.

Now that we have defined each component in our information-processing
model, we are ready to consider how information moves through the system.
Information from the surrounding environment is perceived and recorded by
one of our sense organs. After being perceived by our sense organs, the
information is transmitted to the central processing unit. One very interesting aspect of our sense organs is that they do not transmit all of the information they perceive to the central processing unit. Instead, they transmit only
information which is, in some sense, important. The information which is not
considered important is recorded by the sense receptors for only a very brief
time; it decays quickly unless it is subjected to further processing.

The idea that we process only important information implies that some
mechanism exists which monitors all incoming information and selects the
important parts of that information for further processing—and indeed this
seems to be the case. The available evidence indicates that the central processing unit is constantly monitoring the information perceived by our sense organs.
Information which it considers important is passed on for further processing,
and information not considered important is allowed to decay.

Let's consider an example of this selective processing activity which many of us have experienced. Imagine you are at a crowded cocktail party having a conversation with another person. All around you are people who are also talking, and the noise level generated by all of these people is very high. If we were to ask you what you were attending to (processing) in this situation, you would probably say you were attending only to the person to whom you were talking, and you were ignoring (not processing) the conversations of others around you. You would undoubtedly be correct in this observation, since it would be unlikely that you would be able to recall any of the things the other people were saying. However, imagine that someone nearby mentioned your name. Wham! Most likely, your attention would immediately shift, and you would begin eavesdropping on (processing) the other conversation. This example, conveniently called the "cocktail party phenomenon," suggests that we do monitor all of the information perceived by our sense organs and that we then selectively choose only the important parts of that information for further processing.

1. Why do you think that it is important that we process only part of the information perceived by our sense organs? Why not process all of the information we perceive?

    _____

    _____

    _____

    _____

- - - - - - - - - - - - - - - - - - -

We can handle only so much information. Think of the staggering amount of information we encounter in a single day. If we had to process and store every sight, sound, smell, and touch we encounter, the human information processing system, as wonderful as it is, would surely bog down under the load.

After information has been perceived by the sense organs and passed on as important for further processing, it is transmitted to the central processing unit. The central processing unit then makes a very rapid search of long-term memory to determine if any existing knowledge structure contains information directly relevant to the incoming information. If the incoming information is relevant to information stored in long-term memory, then it is transmitted to long-term memory and integrated into the established knowledge structure. For example, if we told you that Harry Truman was the only president in recent history who was not graduated from college, your central processing unit would make a rapid search of long-term memory, discover that you possess a knowledge structure containing information about President Truman, and then integrate the new fact into the previously established structure.

---

2. Why do you think that it is important to conceptualize the storage process as being selective? Why couldn't information just be stored randomly in memory rather than being stored with related information?

_____

_____

_____

_____

_____

- - - - - - - - - - - - - - - - - - -

We can easily imagine a system where information is stored randomly. However, to imagine how information could be retrieved from such a system is difficult. If information about Harry Truman were haphazardly mixed with all of the other knowledge you possess, how would you ever find a particular bit of knowledge that you wanted to recall? The fact that we can very quickly retrieve isolated bits of information strongly suggests that the retrieval process does not involve a random search of memory. Rather, it suggests that we go to a particular location in memory and look for the information there.

But what happens when incoming information cannot be related to an existing knowledge structure? In that instance, the central processing unit makes a decision about what type of information is being considered. It sorts information into two general types: information from which we can extract a general meaning, and information which must be recalled in exactly the form in which it was experienced.

Let's examine the first type. Imagine going to a lecture on Cognitive Learning Theory when you knew little about learning theories and virtually nothing about Cognitive Learning Theory. After the lecture, you would be able to relate the general sense or the gist of what was said. You would not be able to provide a verbatim word-by-word recitation of the lecture. In this case, you have stored the general meaning of the information but not its exact form.

When the central processing unit encounters information from which we can extract a general meaning, but the information cannot be related to an existing knowledge structure, the information is stored in a newly established structure in long-term memory. One characteristic of information which requires storage in a newly established structure is that our ability to recall such information is poor, relative to our ability to recall information which can be related to previously established knowledge structures. As we will see, this fact has some implications for applying Cognitive Learning Theory to educational problems.

---

3. What explanations can you think of for the fact that we can more easily recall information which is related to something we already know than we can recall something which is new to us?

_____

_____

_____

_____

- - - - - - - - - - - - - - - - - - -

Two explanations are possible. First, information that requires storage in a new structure is stored less well (perhaps less strongly) than information which can be integrated into old structures. This explanation assumes that when we search our memory, we are more likely to be able to find a high-strength bit of information than a low-strength one. The second possibility is that both kinds of information are stored with equal strength in memory, but retrieving (finding) information from a newly established structure is more difficult. Perhaps we have strong retrieval "paths," or even _more_ retrieval paths, to old knowledge structures but weak paths (because they have been used less) to newly established structures. We cannot determine at the present time which of these explanations is correct. However, the available evidence seems to favor the second explanation.

4. As we noted earlier, learning theorists assume that long-term memory has has an unlimited capacity and that once information is stored in long-term memory, it is remembered permanently. How could the theorists assume permanent storage when everyone knows that humans forget?

_____

_____

_____

_____

- - - - - - - - - - - - - - - - - - - -

Retrieval is again the culprit. The information may be stored, but it cannot be found. Some evidence supports this assumption, though to date it is not conclusive.

We have just discussed what happens to information which cannot be related to existing knowledge but from which we can extract a general meaning. The second type of information which might be present when a search of long-term memory reveals no related knowledge structure is information from which we cannot extract a general meaning. Information of this kind requires storage in the exact form in which it is perceived. Names, dates, and telephone numbers are examples of this type of information. For example, to think of the general meaning of someone's name makes little sense. We either know the name or we don't.

Information which requires storage in exact form is difficult to get into long-term memory and requires special processing. Therefore, information of this type is transmitted by the central processing unit to short-term memory which carries out these special processing activities. Earlier in this section we mentioned that short-term memory has both a limited capacity and a limited storage duration. Several years ago, George Miller, a psychologist, suggested that the number "7" had some rather "magical" properties as it relates to human memory. In fact, seven is about the number of units of information we can hold in short-term memory at any given time.

---

5. This question is actually an exercise. Write down a series of random digit strings (for example, 4, 6, 1, 7, 9, 5) consisting of strings with four digits, five digits, six digits, seven digits, eight digits, and nine digits. Then read the digit strings one by one to your friends or classmates at a rate of about one second per digit. After you have read the last digit in each string, ask your listeners to recall the digits in the order in which they were presented.

- - - - - - - - - - - - - - - - -

You should find that most people can recall strings up to six or seven digits with ease. However, only a relatively few people can perfectly recall many more than seven digits. This exercise demonstrates the limited storage capacity of short-term memory.

In addition to limited capacity, short-term memory also has a limited storage duration. We have all had the experience of looking up a telephone number in the telephone directory and beginning to dial the number, only to discover that we have forgotten the number. Experiments on short-term memory have revealed that most information, unless subjected to further processing, will decay after fifteen seconds.

---

6. This experiment will further demonstrate the limited storage duration of short-term memory. Make up a series of three-letter nonsense syllables (for example, MXV, FQP, RZB), and print the syllables (called trigrams) on 3 x 5 cards. Present the card for about one second to a friend or

classmate. As soon as the one-second period is up, remove the card and say a three digit number. Ask your subject to begin counting backward from that number by threes. After about fifteen seconds, stop your subject's counting and ask for recall of the trigram. You should find that your subjects are unable to recall most of the trigrams correctly. If you want to determine the relationship between time and the ability to recall the trigrams, you can vary the amount of time which passes befor you ask for recall. For example, you could ask for recall after five seconds, ten seconds, and fifteen seconds. You should find that the short the period of counting backwards by threes, the better able your subjects are to recall the trigrams.

In this exercise, what is the purpose of having your subjects count backwards by threes?

_____

_____

_____

_____

- - - - - - - - - - - - - - - - - -

To prevent them from further processing the trigrams. The most commc kind of further processing is to say the trigrams over and over (rehears-ing), If allowed to say the trigrams to themselves, subjects can retain the information in short-term memory indefinitely.

Information requiring exact recall must be actively rehearsed in short-term memory before it can be transferred to long-term memory. Therefore, the function of short-term memory is to allow active processing (rehearsal) of information which requires exact recall until that information can be trans-ferred to long-term memory. So, for example, when you move and acquire a new phone number, you have to repeat that number to yourself many times before you can remember it. Likewise, as children we all had to invest hours of practice in learning the multiplication tables.

We have now traced how information is processed and stored in the huma memory system. When important information is perceived by the sense recep tors, it is transferred to the central processing unit. The central processing unit rapidly searches long-term memory to determine if any information relevant to the incoming information is already stored. If so, the incoming information is integrated into these existing knowledge structures. If not, the central processing unit determines which type of information is incoming. If the incoming information is the type that we can extract general meaning from a new knowledge structure for the information is established in long-term memory. If the information is the type which requires exact recall, it is transferred to short-term memory where, after a period of active rehearsal, it is transferred to long-term memory.

To complete our overview of Cognitive Learning Theory, we will consider how the retrieval process works. The recall of previously stored information follows many of the same steps which are involved in the storage process. The request for recall is perceived by our sense receptors and then transferred to the central processing unit. The central processing unit rapidly searches long-term memory (or perhaps short-term memory, if the information has just been learned) to determine if any relevant knowledge structures contain the desired information. If relevant knowledge structures are found in this initial rapid search, a slower, more thorough search is implemented for the required information. As an example of this process, consider what you do while answer-answering the following three questions:

What was the name of Leon Czolgosz's wife?
What was the name of Abraham Lincoln's wife?
What was the name of Lyndon Johnson's wife?

Chances are that when you read the first question, you drew a complete blank and didn't even both to search through memory for the answer. The decision that you didn't know the answer was probably very fast. The second question probably took considerably more time. You recognized that you know a great deal about Abraham Lincoln and that you were likely to have Mrs. Lincoln's name stored in memory. In fact, many of you probably remembered that Mrs. Lincoln's name was Mary. With the third question, you probably had yet another experience. You probably felt that you knew the answer, since Johnson's wife is frequently in the news; you had merely to search through memory until you came up with Lady Bird. Incidently, Leon Czolgosz was the man who assassinated President William McKinley, and he didn't have a wife!

The likelihood that a search of long-term memory will result in the successful retrieval of information depends on two factors. First, recently learned information is much more likely to be recalled than information learned in the distant past. And, second, information integrated into well-established (frequently used) knowledge structures is much more likely to be recalled than information integrated into less-established knowledge structures. For example, consider your own course work. The chances are that you can better remember information from courses within your major than from courses outside your major. Knowledge structures formed from major coursework are probably richer, more elaborate, and more frequently used than are structures formed in less related courses.

ASSUMPTIONS UNDERLYING COGNITIVE LEARNING THEORY

We are now ready to consider the basic assumptions underlying Cognitive Learning Theory, compared to those underlying applied Operant Learning Theory and Associative Learning Theory. Perhaps the most striking aspect of Cognitive Learning Theory is the degree to which humans are considered to be active processors of incoming stimulus information.

In both applied Operant Learning Theory and Associative Learning Theory humans are viewed as relatively passive recorders and processors of environmental events. In applied Operant Learning Theory a person experiences an external stimulus and responds to it. The environmental consequences (that is, reward or punishment) following that event determine whether the response is likely to occur again in the presenece of the stimulus. To predict what a person will do in any given situation we need to know the stimulus events the person has experienced, the responses made in the presence of those events, and the consequences which followed the responses. All of these events occur external to the person experiencing them. Applied Operant Learning Theory says very little about processes occuring inside the person.

In Associative Learning Theory, too, the person is viewed as a relatively passive recorder of external events. In Associative Learning Theory the person forms associative bonds between stimulus and response events through encountering those events at the same time. Note that in Associative Learning Theory the mere contiguous occurrence of stimulus and response events is sufficient for learning to occur, whereas in applied Operant Learning Theory a consequence must follow the events. However, in Associative Learning Theory we again need only to know about external events in order to describe the learning process. The person is viewed simply as a passive recorder of those events.

In contrast, Cognitive Learning Theory does not view the learner as merely a passive recorder of external events. Instead, the learner is viewed as a very active participant in the learning process. Events occurring within the person are responsible for (1) deciding what information is important enough to deserve further processing; (2) deciding whether information relevant to incoming information is already stored in memory; (3) deciding whether information should be stored in general meaning form'or exact form; (4) determining the storage location for incoming information; and (5) conducting a search process which retrieves stored information from memory.

At the present time the assumptions underlying these three theories are best viewed as competing perspectives on the nature of the human learning process. Future research may establish one perspective as more valid than the others, or it may established that the most valid perspective combines elements from all of the theories. However, we need not determine which theory is most valid in order for the theories to be useful in educational situations. As we have seen, different theories can prove useful with different kinds of problems. The teacher who is familiar with all three theories and can translate the theories into educational practice has a valuable tool for solving learning problems.

7. Sigmund Freud developed a theory of human behavior which examined a number of ideas concerning human memory. One aspect of the theory suggested that memory consisted of two parts: a conscious memory which contained events and experiences of a nontraumatic nature, and a subconscious memory where traumatic (psychologically painful) events and

experiences were stored. Freud suggested that the events and experiences stored in conscious memory were readily available for recall. However, events in subconscious memory could be recalled only through intensive therapeutic experiences. Based on what you just read about the basic assumptions underlying the three learning theories, which theory would you judge to be most similar to Freudian theory? Why?

_____

_____

_____

_____

- - - - - - - - - - - - - - - - - -

Freudian theory is most consistent with the assumptions underlying Cognitive Learning Theory. The view that we direct the storage of some kinds of events to one type of memory and other kinds of events to a different type of memory is consistent with the assumption that humans are active processors of information, rather than passive recorders of events.

SITUATIONS IN WHICH COGNITIVE LEARNING THEORY MIGHT BE APPLIED

Cognitive Learning Theory is most appropriately applied in situations where students are having difficulty with complex learning and complex learning skills. Complex learning is best defined by contrasting it with simple, or rote, learning. When we memorize facts, learn to perform skills in a specified sequence, or acquire vocabulary words in a foreign language, we are engaging in simple, rote learning. To specify the desired end product of the rote learning activity is relatively easy. Rote learning plays an important, even critical, part in the educational process. Much of what we can do as educated adults rests upon a foundation of basic skills learned by rote.

However, the acquisition of skills learned by rote forms only a portion of the goal of education. The other aspect of the educational goal is to educate students to be able critically to evaluate information they encounter and to understand new subject matter. Cognitive Learning Theory is directed toward teaching students to think about and to understand the material they encounter. The end product of complex learning is much more difficult to specify than that of rote learning. Much more ingenuity is required on a teacher's part to determine that students have mastered a complex learning skill than to determine that they have mastered a simple skill or learned a fact by rote. In this section we will consider how a teacher can recognize a situation where an educational problem involves complex learning or the performance of a complex learning skill.

When <u>students</u> <u>cannot</u> <u>apply</u> <u>previously</u> <u>learned</u> <u>information</u> <u>to</u> <u>a</u> <u>new,</u> <u>but</u>
<u>related,</u> <u>example,</u> complex learning is a problem. For example, let's assume
that in a science class you were teaching, you were exploring the physical
properties of materials. In a discussion of the hardness of various materials,
you mentioned that iron was harder than copper, that glass was harder than
iron (even though it is more brittle), and that diamonds were harder than glass.
On a subsequent test, you asked the students, "What material would you use
to cut glass?" Virtually all of the students were unable to answer this question
and in a subsequent discussion with the students about their test performance,
you heard the familiar student complaint, "How are we supposed to know that?
You never taught us the answer!"

The inability of students to apply learned information generally occurs
because of one (or both) of two problems. The first problem is that students
may know information, in the sense that they can recite it, but they really
don't <u>understand</u> the information. For example, the authors of this book know
that the relationship between energy, mass, and velocity is characterized by
the formula $E = MC^2$, but in little sense can we say that we really understand
this relationship. If we really understood the relationship, we could use that
understanding as a conceptual tool for explaining events in the natural world
around us. In the same sense, students can often master academic information
to the extent that they can feed it back to a teacher; still, they have not mastered an understanding of that information which would allow them to apply it
to a new situation.

We think of understanding as the process of integrating newly acquired
information into previously established knowledge structures. Thus, when
information is comprehended and understood, it becomes part of a richly
elaborated network consisting of events, facts, and abstract conceptual knowledge. In contrast, when information is learned but not understood, it is stored
in essentially the same form in which it was experienced. As a result, it is of
little use when the task at hand calls for more than direct recall of the
information.

When students are unable to apply learned information to new situations
and are willing to exert the effort necessary for understanding, the problem
may be that for one reason or another they are unable to integrate the new
information into an existing knowledge structure. The second problem might
occur when students do not exert the cognitive effort necessary to attain
understanding.

Much of the information we learn on a daily basis requires little cognitive
effort to acquire. Information which can be related to things we already know
is easily learned and easily understood. However, some kinds of information
we learn require cognitive effort to be understood. For example, suppose that
we told you that to achieve a high-gloss finish on a piece of furniture, you must
scratch the surface of the finish. Your first reaction to this statement is likely
to be disbelief; even if you believe the statement, you may not understand it.
Then, upon reflection (cognitive effort!), you may realize that polishing a surface involves eroding away large surface blemishes by inflicting thousands of
minute uniform scratches on the finished surface. The smaller the scratches,
the more glossy and smooth the surface appears to the eye.

When their tasks require recall, but not application, of learned information, students can easily get out of (or never learn) the habit of making the cognitive effort necessary to achieve understanding. Much of the educational content of early elementary-level schooling involves the mastery of basic skills. By necessity, the students' tasks at this level involve frequent practice and recall of these basic skills. All too frequently, however, the practice of requiring only recall of information continues into upper grade levels where students should be obtaining experience in using information rather than just learning it for recall. If for years students experience only recall tasks, they often get into the habit of learning the material so that they can feed it back, rather than learning it for application to new situations. Learning new, unfamiliar information so that it can be used requires integration of the information into existing knowledge structures, and this integration process requires conscious, cognitive effort.

In summary, Cognitive Learning Theory is applicable where students are unable to apply what they have learned to new problems or situations. Two events could be responsible for this failure. First, the students may be unable to integrate the information into existing knowledge structures and therefore, may be unable to "understand" it. Second, they may not have exerted the cognitive effort necessary to carry out the integration process.

8. Ms. Carter teaches a high school biology class which, among other things, studies the structure of living cells. In her final exam she presents the class with a diagram of a cell and asks the students to label the parts. To her dismay, most of the students are unable to label the parts correctly. Is this a situation calling for the use of Cognitive Learning Theory? Why, or why not?

Cognitive Learning Theory would not be appropriate in this instance. The task involves direct recall of information rather than application of information. Associative Learning Theory would be a much more appropriate choice.

9. Mr. Wilson teaches a high school biology class in which he spends a portion of classtime on the study of genetics. In the course he has discussed the genetic theory on heredity, and he has spent considerable time on the concept of dominant and recessive genes. Recall tests for this material had indicated that the students had mastered this material to the point where they could reproduce it on tests. Near the end of the semester, Mr. Wilson decided to conduct an experiment. He and his students crossed a pea plant having a white flower with a pea plant having a red flower (sound familiar?). Before these new pea plants began to flower, Mr. Wilson

asked his class to predict what color flower the new plants would have. Every student in the class predicted that the new plants would have pink flowers! Is this a situation calling for the use of Cognitive Learning Theory? Why, or why not?

_____

_____

_____

- - - - - - - - - - - - - - - - - - - -

Yes, it is. As you may remember from Mendel's experiments, flower color in pea plants is determined by dominant and recessive genes, with red dominant. If the red parent plant had two red genes, the flowers of the resulting plants will be all red. If the red parent plant had one red gene and one white gene, some of the resulting plants would have red flowers, and some would have white flowers. The white parent plant woul of course, have two white genes.

The fact that the students predicted pink flowers indicates that even though the students are able to state verbally the essentials of genetic theory, they have not understood the theory to the point where they can use it to make predictions about unfamiliar events. Cognitive Learning Theory is useful in precisely this kind of situation.

PRINCIPLES IN APPLYING COGNITIVE LEARNING THEORY
TO EDUCATIONAL PROBLEMS

Two general principles derived from Cognitive Learning Theory can be applie to educational problems of the kind we have discussed. First, as teachers, we should provide our students with frequent practice in using information, as well as requiring recall. As we have just discussed, students often fail in applying learned information to a new situation, because they have not exerted the cognitive effort necessary to really understand the material. When student have a long educational history of being asked to recall material and little experience in being asked to use it, they simply memorize it for recall. We can remedy this situation by providing our students with frequent practice in both recalling and using the information we present.

10. In Ms. Brauch's math class the students are learning how to compute the area of a rectangle. What questions or exercises can you think of which would give the students practice in using the information they are learning

_____

_____

_____

You may have mentioned several of the many possibilities. Several we thought of are:

a. Assume we wanted to lay a wall-to-wall carpet in our classroom. How large a rug would we order from the rug company?
b. Which is larger, the space contained on our football field or the space underneath our school building?
c. If you removed all of the seats from a school bus, could you pack more students into the school bus than you could pack into the school principal's office?

The idea behind providing students with frequent practice in applying information is that, after a period of time, the students will get into the habit of relating new information to what they already know. And if they routinely relate new information to old they will be much better able to apply the learned information when appropriate.

A word of caution is in order. Many teachers provide their students with practice in applying information by providing them with academic exercises they have never seen before. This type of application procedure is unnecessarily limited. Students who frequently encounter situations where they are asked to apply learned information to academic exercises can easily develop the attitude that the "stuff" they learn in school is useful only for solving academic problems. Teachers should make a conscious effort to select application problems which demonstrate that the newly learned information is relevant to the solution of real-world problems. While it takes more time and ingenuity to think of real-world applications, the payoff is worth the effort. Many of the concerns we hear about "educational relevancy" would vanish if all teachers made a conscientious effort to show the utility of school learning in the real world.

The second principle of applying Cognitive Learning Theory to educational problems is that new information should be presented so that it can be connected with and integrated into a previously established knowledge structure. Let's consider a simple demonstration which illustrates this principle. Assume you heard the sentence, "The notes were sour because the seams were split." Chances are that you were puzzled by this sentence. You could memorize the sentence if we asked you to do so, but you are probably having difficulty understanding what the sentence means. From the perspective of Cognitive Learning Theory, the reason that you can't understand this sentence is that you can't

relate it to anything you already know. That is, you cannot integrate the information into existing knowledge structures.

Now watch what happens when we give you a single word: Bagpipe! You
have probably experienced an immediate sense of comprehension. This demonstration makes the point that some information we encounter is very difficult
to understand if we cannot relate it to something we already know. Further,
students are likely to encounter this situation rather frequently, since they are
continually being introduced to new and unfamiliar material. They may learn
this material to the point where they can reproduce it, but they may not really
understand it.

To maximize the likelihood that students will understand the material we
present to them, we should point out the relationship between the new material
and previously learned material. One very powerful and effective way to establish relationships is through the frequent use of analogies. An analogy is a
statement which indicates that one thing or event is similar to another. For
example, if we were describing a rhea—a large two-toed bird that lives in
South America—you might have some difficulty conceptualizing what the bird
looks like. However, if we told you that a rhea looks much like an ostrich but
is slightly smaller, you would probably have a much better sense of the bird's
appearance. Notice that in this example we used knowledge you almost certainly
have (what an ostrich looks like) as an aid to understanding new information
(what a rhea looks like).

Teachers can use analogies in a similar fashion. The internal structure of
an atom, for example, could be presented as being analogous to the solar system, with the sun being compared to the nucleus of the atom and the electrons
orbiting the nucleus being analogous to the planets orbiting the sun. In this
example we are again using information which the students already know as an
aid to understanding new information.

---

11. Assume you wanted to explain to your students how the human eye works.
    How could you begin your explanation so that your students would be likely
    to understand the material you are presenting?

    _____

    _____

    _____

- - - - - - - - - - - - - - - - - - -

    You could point out that the human eye is analogous to a camera. The
    retina of the eye has some similarities to the film in a camera, the pupil
    of the eye is similar to a camera lens, and so on.

TECHNIQUES IN APPLYING COGNITIVE LEARNING THEORY

REVIEW

12. Earlier in this chapter we mentioned that students' failure to understand material may result from one of two reasons. What are the two reasons?

_____

_____

_____

_____

- - - - - - - - - - - - - - - - - -

1. Lack of cognitive effort. Students frequently fail to exert the cognitive effort necessary to understand new material. Instead they simply memorize the material so it can be recalled later.
2. Lack of conceptual understanding. Students may fail to understand new material because they cannot relate the material to information they already know. That is, they cannot integrate the material into existing knowledge structures.

The techniques involved in applying Cognitive Learning Theory are designed to remedy the two situations mentioned above. To stimulate cognitive effort, we want to provide students with frequent practice in using information as well as in recalling it. Two practice methods are available. First, as we've discussed, you may present the information you would like your students to acquire, and then ask your students to solve problems or answer questions which require the application of the information to situations they have not encountered before. The second way to encourage cognitive effort involves a formalized teaching procedure called Discovery Learning.

The basic idea in a Discovery Learning approach to teaching is that the students are presented with a series of examples carefully constructed to show a particular concept or principle in operation and are then led to discover the concept or principle for themselves. As an example of a Discovery Learning approach, let's see if you can discover the psychological principle involved in the following three stories. Examine the stories carefully, and pay particular attention to the commonalities in the stories. After examining the stories, see if you can discover the common principle that accounts for the events in all of the stories.

Story 1. Professor Micah drives an old Hudson Hornet which he dearly loves, but the car is terribly unreliable. About one out of every three times he gets into the car, it doesn't start. When it fails to start, he gets out and shakes various things, mutters a few words of endearment to "Huddy Baby," and tries again. Occasionally he is rewarded for these activities, because the car starts. One particular cold winter morning, he goes out to the car and

attempts to start it. When it doesn't start, he begins to pat the dashboard
while frantically pumping the gas. When that doesn't work, he gets out of the
car, opens the hood, and shakes the air filter a couple of times. He then gets
back in the car and tries again. After about one-half hour of puttering around,
he finally gives up and marches out to the street to try to hitch a ride with a
friendly motorist.

Professor Manycents teaches in the same department as Professor Micah.
During the summer he bought a brand new foreign sports car and one of the
things he finds rewarding about owning the car is that it starts every time he
turns the key. On the same cold morning that Professor Micah had his difficulties, Professor Manycents goes out to his car and discovers that it won't
start. After about ten minutes of grinding the motor, he gives up in disgust
and walks away, muttering about lousy foreign products.

Story 2. Homer the chipmunk lives in a wilderness area which campers
and fishermen visit throughout the summer. During the summer, Homer goes
down to a campsite where the visitors camp and scours the area for tidbits the
have left. Occasionally, he finds a juicy scrap which he devours with relish.
When the fall comes, and the area has been closed to visitors, he continues to
visit the campsite for several weeks, looking in vain for bits of food.

Harry the chipmunk lives under a cabin by the lake. During the summer
he makes friends with a little girl who lives in the cabin. Every morning she
comes out with a pocket full of crunchy little nuggets which taste just like wild
hickory nuts to Harry. When the little girl leaves at the end of the summer,
for two days Harry visits the rock where the girl has fed him and then moves
out of his burrow under the cabin and goes in search of greener pastures.

Story 3. Bessie Strongarm has read in the paper that the psychology
department at the local university is conducting an experiment which involves
playing a slot machine. Since she loves playing slot machines, she immediate
rushes over to sign up as a subject. In the room where the experiment is bein
conducted, she is given a roll of pennies and directed to a machine. She is tol
that she can keep all of the money that she wins from the games. (What Bessie
doesn't know is that the machine is scheduled to pay her two pennies on the
average for every time she pulls the handle. "On the average" means that son
times Bessie gets nothing for her pull, but sometimes she gets many pennies
in return. But if we were to average the number of pennies per pull, it would
come out to two). After an hour the machine pays no more pennies. Bessie
continues to play the machine until she has lost all of her pennies.

John Pinchpants reads the same advertisement and also signs up to be a
subject in the experiment. However, his machine is programmed to pay him
two pennies on every pull. As was the case with Bessie, after an hour the
machine no longer pays any pennies. After putting about twelve pennies into
the machine and receiving nothing in return, John goes home with his winnings

13. What principle accounts for the events in the three stories?

_____

_____

_____

- - - - - - - - - - - - - - - - -

Your principle should be stated in words similar to these: If reward or reinforcement occurs only occasionally following a particular behavior, the behavior will continue for a long period of time after the reward stops. If reward follows every time a behavior is performed, the behavior will only persist for a short period of time after the reward stops. By the way, the principle works in practice. Ask any casino owner in Las Vegas.

Several features of Discovery Learning make the approach highly consistent with the goals and principles of Cognitive Learning Theory. To discover the principle behind the stories we just presented, you had to take a highly active cognitive role. You stored the essential details of each story, retrieved these details to compare one story with another, and generated a principle which would account for the events in each of the stories. Each of these activities involves an interplay between new information and information already stored in memory. Further, each of these activities involved cognitive effort which very likely led you to understand the principle better than you would have if we had simply told you the principle.

The second type of situation to which Cognitive Learning Theory techniques might be applied is when students have difficulty in understanding new material because they cannot relate it to anything they already know. This type of problem poses limits to solution. For example, the vast majority of us could not pick up a scientific journal and read its contents with a high level of understanding. We simply do not have the relevant background knowledge which would be necessary for understanding. Fortunately, however, most information we present to our students does not require such a high level of background knowledge in order to be understood. In any case, understanding will generally be enhanced if you simply point out the relationship between the new material and previously learned material.

As an exercise in relating new material to previously learned material, let's assume we want to teach our students why metals are particularly good conductors of electricity. As it happens, metals have two properties which make them very good electrical conductors. First, metals have an abundance of free-floating electrons; second, they have a highly regular (crystalline) molecular structure. An abundance of free-floating electrons is important because current flow involves the movement of electrons through the conducting material. Without free electrons, current flow cannot occur. The regular structure of the material is important, because it allows a relatively unimpeded passage of the electrons through the material. In contrast, if a material has a highly irregular molecular structure, the electrons collide with the molecules (few free "passages" of the entire length of the material occur), and a few electrons successfully pass through the material.

14. Suppose you wanted to teach the above material to one of your classes (which already has a basic understanding of electricity and current flow). How would you present the material so that students could relate it to material they are already familiar with? (Try to think of an example which would be familiar to the students and would illustrate why free-floating electrons and a regular molecular structure are important properties of a good electrical conductor.)

_____

_____

_____

_____

_____

_____

- - - - - - - - - - - - - - - - - - - -

The relationship might be established in many ways. We would choose to present the information in this way:

"Class, today we are going to talk about why metals are good conductors of electricity. But, first, I want you to imagine that you are at the town fair. At the fair are two booths with a game which involves throwing a football through a series of five tires. If you throw three footballs through all five tires within a minute, you win a prize. In one of the two booths, the man operating the game has only two footballs; after you throw the two footballs, he must run to the end of the game booth, pick up the balls, and bring them back to you before you can throw again. In the other booth, the game operator has many footballs, and you can throw one after another until your minute is up. If you could win a prize only after you threw three footballs through the tires within a minute, I'm sure you would rather play the game at the booth with many footballs; correct?

"Now, let's imagine that in the booth with only two footballs, the five tires are lined up a bit irregularly. One tire juts out a little to one side, the next one a little to the other side, and so on. As a result, if we look down through the center of the tires, we can see that the opening through the series of tires is only slightly larger than a football. In contrast, in the booth with many footballs, the five tires are perfectly aligned. The passage through the series of five tires is as large as the hole in the center of each tire.

"Now all of you, I'm sure, would prefer to play the game in the booth with many footballs where the tires are perfectly lined up. The chances that you could throw three footballs through the tires in a minute are much greater at this booth.

"What does this example have to do with metals and current flow? Let's see. Metals are good conductors of electricity for many of the same reasons the booth with more footballs and perfectly aligned tires is preferable to you. First, metals have many free-floating electrons, while other materials have few free electrons. The chances that the electrons will move from one end of a material to the other are much greater when many electrons are present rather than just a few. This situation is similar to the booth where you were more likely to throw several balls through the tires in a given time because more balls were available to be thrown. Metals also have a property relatable to the alignment of the tires. Metals have a highly regular internal structure; that is, all of the molecules in a metal are lined up in rows, and openings between the molecules run the length of the material. In contrast, nonmetals have a very irregular internal structure. Like the irregularity lined-up tires, one molecule juts out here, another there, so that very few open passages run the length of the material. Thus when electrons come shooting down the material, many of them collide with the molecules which block their flow. As a result, few electrons pass the length of the material."

Your answer to the question was probably quite different from the one we present above. The important thing to check for in your answer was whether you related the new information to information the student already knew. In Chapter 6, we will give you the opportunity to practice the skill of relating new information to old in other situations. Chapter 6 will also provide you with practice in applying all of the aspects of Cognitive Learning Theory presented in this chapter.

ADDITIONAL READINGS

Anderson, J. R., and Bower, G. H. Human Associative Memory. Washington, D.C.: V. H. Winston & Sons, 1973.

Carroll, J. B., and Freedle, R. O. (eds.). Language Comprehension and the Acquisition of Knowledge. Washington, D.C.: V. H. Winston & Sons, 1972.

Melton, A. W., and Martin, E. (eds.). Coding Process in Human Memory. Washington, D.C.: V. H. Winston & Sons, 1972.

Neisser, U. Cognitive Psychology. New York: Appleton-Century-Crofts, 1967.

Saltz, E. The Cognitive Bases of Human Learning. Homewood, Illinois: The Dorsey Press, 1971.

Solso, R. L. (ed.). Contemporary Issues in Cognitive Psychology: The Loyola Symposium. Washington, D.C.: V. H. Winston & Sons, 1973.

Tulving, E., and Donaldson, W. (eds.). Organization of Memory. New York: Academic Press, 1972.

Weimer, W. B., and Palermo, D. S. (eds.). Cognition and the Symbolic Processes. Hillsdale, New Jersey: Lawrence Erlbaum Associates, 1974.

SELF-TEST

This self-test is designed to show you whether or not you have mastered the objectives of Chapter 5. Answer each question to the best of your ability, based on what you learned in this chapter. Correct answers are given following the test.

1. Listed below are the elements of the model of human information processing presented in Chapter 5. Briefly define each of the following elements.

   a. Incoming information: _____

   _____

   b. Sense receptors: _____

   _____

   c. Central processing unit: _____

   _____

   d. Short-term memory: _____

   _____

   e. Long-term memory: _____

   _____

   f. Response generator: _____

   _____

   g. Response output: _____

   _____

2. Fill in the model of human information processing on the following page. Make sure that each of the elements listed in Question 1 is in the correct position.

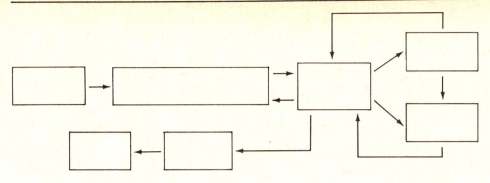

3. How are the assumptions or principles underlying Cognitive Learning Theory different from those underlying applied Operant Learning Theory and Associative Learning Theory?

_____

_____

_____

_____

_____

4. For each situation described below, circle whether applied Operant Learning Theory (O), Associative Learning Theory (A), or Cognitive Learning Theory (C) should be used.

   O   A   C   a. Mr. Smith is having difficulty teaching his class the basic vocabulary used in describing economic theory.

   O   A   C   b. Ms. Brown wants her class to use geographical concepts to analyze topography and to hypothesize where cities would grow up.

   O   A   C   c. Bill Ortega wants to learn the procedures for making papier-mâché figures.

   O   A   C   d. Ms. Swenson cannot get three members of her class to do their homework assignments.

   O   A   C   e. Mr. Reinhard wishes his class could use the mathematics knowledge they have learned to solve practical problems in everyday life.

   O   A   C   f. Susan Carlotte will not pay attention in class frequently enough to understand the presentations.

5. List the two basic principles involved in applying Cognitive Learning Theory to an educational problem.

a. _____

_____

_____

b. _____

_____

6. Describe the two techniques to be used in applying Cognitive Learning Theory to educational situations.

a. _____

_____

_____

b. _____

_____

_____

ANSWERS TO SELF-TEST

Compare your answers to the questions on the self-test with the answers given below. If all of your answers are correct, you are ready to go on to the next chapter. If you missed any questions, review the appropriate parts of the chapter before you go on.

1. a. Incoming information: Any information we receive in our environment.

    b. Sense receptors: The organs which receive the incoming information.

    c. Central processing unit: The unit that decides how to process information.

    d. Short-term memory: The area which stores information for a brief period of time—about fifteen seconds.

    e. Long-term memory: The area which stores information for an unlimited amount of time.

    f. Response generator: The systems that allow us to interact with our environment.

    g. Response output: The output from the response generator, such as speaking, acting, or thinking.

2.

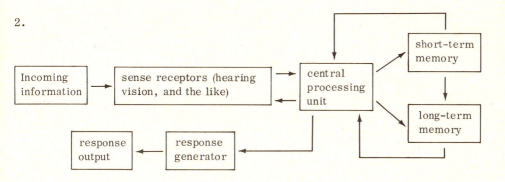

3. Applied Operant Learning Theory and Associative Learning Theory assume the participant to be passive in the learning process, while Cognitive Learning Theory assumes the participant as being actively involved in the learning process.

4. a. A

    b. C

    c. A

    d. O

      e.   C

      f.   O

5.   a.   Provide students with frequent practice in using the information they are learning.

      b.   Integrate new information into a previously established knowledge structure.

6.   a.   Provide students with frequent practice in applying new knowledge in a variety of settings. This technique is particularly useful where the students' problem is lack of cognitive effort.

      b.   Use discovery learning, where the students work through problem situations to "discover" the concepts or principles you wish them to learn. This technique is especially useful when the students' problem is lack of conceptual understanding, because it helps students relate new information to known information.

CHAPTER SIX

Application of Cognitive Learning Theory to Educational Problems

In Chapter 5 we discussed the basic principles underlying Cognitive Learning Theory and generally how to apply the theory to educational problems. In this chapter we will give you some practice in designing a Cognitive Learning approach.

After completing this chapter, you should be able to:

1. Identify educational problems to which Cognitive Learning Theory could be applied.
2. Determine if an educational problem involves a lack of cognitive effort or a lack of conceptual understanding.
3. Design a Cognitive Learning Theory approach to an educational problem.

IDENTIFYING SITUATIONS WHERE COGNITIVE LEARNING THEORY IS APPROPRIATE

In Chapter 5 we indicated that Cognitive Learning Theory could be appropriately applied where students cannot apply learned information to unfamiliar situations. Before determining whether Cognitive Learning Theory can be applied to a given problem, you must first ascertain whether the students have mastered the material they are being asked to apply. If they have not, then Cognitive Learning Theory may not be the most useful learning theory to apply. Instead you would probably apply Associative Learning Theory. However, where students have mastered the basic material but are still unable to apply the learned information to new situations, Cognitive Learning Theory is a proper approach. Let's practice identifying some of these situations.

1. James Mitchell is a kindergarten teacher who has been teaching Martha, one of the students in his class, to tell time from the classroom clock. After Mr. Mitchell has worked periodically with Martha for several weeks,

she is able to look at the clock and give him the correct time when he asks for it. One day at recess, Mr. Mitchell walks over to Martha, shows her his wristwatch, and asks her, "What time is it?" She answers, "It's one o'clock in the morning." Could we apply Cognitive Learning Theory to this situation? Why, or why not?

_____

_____

_____

_____

_____

- - - - - - - - - - - - - - - - - - -

Yes. Martha has mastered the skill of telling time from the classroom clock, but she cannot _transfer_ that skill to a new situation. In other words, she cannot apply the learned skill when asked to do so.

2. Herman Hoffer is a ninth grader who aspires to become a great mathematician. As an initial step toward that goal, he has asked Mr. Wundt, his math teacher, if he may do independent study in advanced algebra. Mr. Wundt lends him one of his college algebra textbooks, and Herman spends the semester working through the text. At the end of the semester, Herman informs Mr. Wundt that he has matered all of the material in the text. As a check on Herman's mastery, Mr. Wundt selects several problems from the text that Herman has been studying and asks Herman to solve them. Out of the ten problems Mr. Wundt has selected, Herman can solve only two. Would Cognitive Learning Theory be appropriately applied to this problem? Why, or why not?

_____

_____

_____

_____

_____

- - - - - - - - - - - - - - - - - - -

No. The problems that Herman could not solve were taken directly from the text he had been studying. The problem seems to be a failure to master basic algebraic skills, rather than an inability to apply learned knowledge.

3. Mr. Jay teaches a social studies course which examines the governmental structure of the United States. On one of his exams, he asks the question: "Which branch of the government is responsible for determining if a particular law is in accordance with the Constitution of the United States?"

The majority of the students in the class miss the question. Might Cognitive Learning Theory be appropriate to this situation? Why, or why not?

_____

_____

_____

_____

- - - - - - - - - - - - - - - - - -

Cognitive Learning Theory would not be appropriate. The question asks for the recall of a fact rather than the application of learned material to a new situation. Associative Learning Theory would be more appropriate.

4. Mr. Newton is teaching his high school plysics class about gravitational force. After spending some time on this topic, on an exam he asks his students the following two questions: "(1) What is the formula for the acceleration of an object when dropped from the Empire State Building?" and "(2) If a steel ball and a feather were dropped from the same height in a vacuum, which would reach the ground first?" The class were uniformly successful in answering the first question, but almost everyone said the steel ball would hit the ground before the feather. Would Cognitive Learning Theory we appropriate in this situation? Why, or why not?

_____

_____

_____

_____

_____

- - - - - - - - - - - - - - - - - -

Yes. The students have mastered a formula which predicts the velocity of a falling object, but they do not realize that in a frictionless environment (one with no air), the mass of an object is irrelevant to its velocity. Incidently, some of you may remember that one of the astronauts performed the experiment described in Mr. Newton's question. The astronaut dropped a feather and a hammer at the same time onto the surface of the moon. Sure enough, they hit the ground at the same time.

ANALYZING PROBLEMS CALLING FOR THE APPLICATION
OF COGNITIVE LEARNING THEORY

You should now be able to identify those situations where the application of Cognitive Learning Theory would be appropriate. Now we will practice analyzing such educational problems. Specifically, we will focus on determining whether a problem results from a lack of cognitive effort or from a failure in basic understanding.

When students simply memorize information for recall and make little attempt to integrate the newly learned information into previously established knowledge structures, the problem is lack of cognitive effort, which we call poor cognitive habits. The result is that students can reproduce the information they have learned, but they cannot use it.

In reality, teachers are more responsible for poor cognitive habits than are students. The teacher who continually asks students to feed back learned information in the same form is encouraging the students simply to memorize the material. We do not wish to imply that memorization of academic material has no place in our schools. As we mentioned earlier, rote acquisition of information and skills forms the basic foundation for the higher order skills and knowledge acquired later in the schooling process. The danger is that practices which are appropriate for teaching basic skills and knowledge are sometimes continued—inappropriately—in teaching higher order skills and knowledge. For example, we have accomplished little of importance if we ask our students to memorize the fact that each state is represented in the federal government by two senators and a number of representatives, and then find that our students would not know whom to contact to express an opinion on pending legislation.

When students are unable to apply learned information to a new situation, a teacher should first examine his or her own teaching practices. If most of the questions the teacher asks the students (either in classroom discussions or on exams) are direct-recall questions, then student inability to apply learned information to new situations may well be due to poor cognitive habits. That is, the students may have developed the habit of memorizing the material without making the cognitive effort necessary to integrate it into a previously established knowledge structure.

Let's look at an example. Assume that in a social studies course, you were taught that the president of the United States is actually elected by the electoral college. You can do two things when presented with this information. You can simply memorize it for recall, or you can think about its implications. You might think about how each state is allocated a certain number of votes in the electoral college and note that these votes are cast in accordance with the popular vote in that state. Assume that later you learned that in the presidential election of 1876, Rutherford Hayes was elected president after receiving fewer popular votes than Samuel Tilden, his opponent.

If you had simply memorized the fact that presidential elections were determined by the vote of the electoral college, you would be in a relatively poor position to understand how a president could be elected with fewer votes than his opponent. To do so, you would have to search your memory, find the isolated fact about the electoral college, and then infer the relationship between popular votes and electoral college votes. In contrast, if you had thought about this relationship at the time of learning, the fact about the electoral college would be integrated into your knowledge structure concerning popular voting in presidential elections. You could then easily imagine a situation where a candidate could win some states with a very large plurality of votes, lose other states by a very small margin of votes, and end up with more total votes than his opponent but still lose the election in the electoral college.

The above example illustrates the advantage of giving students activities which encourage the cognitive processing necessary to integrate learned information into existing knowledge structures. The next few questions will give you some practice in determining if a teacher is encouraging this kind of activity.

---

5. Mr. Gauss teaches a high school geometry class. He assigns homework on a weekly basis, and he gives four examinations spaced at fairly regular intervals throughout the year. He takes his homework problems from those given at the end of each of the chapters in the book. His exam questions involve a random selection of problems which have previously been given as homework. Is Mr. Gauss encouraging his students to be active cognitive participants in the learning process, or is he encouraging poor cognitive habits? Why?

    _____

    _____

    _____

    _____

    _____

- - - - - - - - - - - - - - - - - -

    Mr. Gauss is clearly encouraging poor cognitive habits in his students. His students would quickly realize that to perform well on the exams they need only memorize the steps and answers in the homework problems. No course requirement encourages active cognitive processing of the material.

6. Having decided that Mr. Gauss is not encouraging his students to actively process the material, how would you suggest that Mr. Gauss change his teaching procedures so that the students were encouraged actively to process the material? Two things should be kept in mind as you develop your recommendations. First, Mr. Gauss would like to be certain that the students have mastered the basic concepts and principles of geometry. Second, Mr. Gauss would like to be sure that these concepts and principles are learned in the most useful form. Thus, Mr. Gauss must establish

that basic skills and concepts have been learned and provide activities which require active cognitive processing of the learned material so that they can be applied to new situations. What are your recommendations?

_____

_____

_____

_____

_____

- - - - - - - - - - - - - - - - - - -

Many possibilities exist. Our recommendations would be as follows: Mr. Gauss' current teaching practices are directed toward trying to make sure that basic concepts and skills have been mastered. As a step toward assuring that these concepts and skills are learned in a useful form, he should pair each recall question with a question which requires the application of that basic skill or concept to a new situation. For example, a question which asks for the recall of the Pythagorean Theorem could be accompanied by a question which asks the students to apply the theorem. Mr. Gauss might, for example, ask the students to use the theorem to compute the height of a building.

7. In a junior high science class, Ms. Wilson spends some time on the origin of pollutants in our atmosphere. She begins her coverage of this topic by discussing the molecular and chemical properties of various fuels. She then goes on to describe how these fuels combine with oxygen during the combustion process to release heat. In addition, she discusses how unburned parts of the fuel and new compounds formed in the combustion process are released into the atmosphere. While covering this topic, Ms. Wilson is very careful to make sure that the students are acquiring the basics of the subject—she gives the students frequent quizzes and asks recall questions in class. Ms. Wilson also asks frequent application questions. For example, she has asked her class if (from the pollution standpoint) propane gas would be a better fuel to burn for the generation of electricity than would coal or fuel oil. In addition, she has asked whether alcohol would be a cleaner burning fuel than gasoline. The difficulty has been that the students do well on the recall of the information, but they have not done well on the application questions. They answer the application questions and sometimes give elaborate reasons for their answers, but their answers are usually erroneous. Are poor cognitive habits responsible for this poor student performance? Why, or why not?

_____

_____

_____

_____
_____
- - - - - - - - - - - - - - - -

No. Ms. Wilson is following teaching practices which encourage the acquisition of basic concepts and skills and the integration of this basic information into existing knowledge structures. The problem seems to be that the students are unable to carry out the integration process. That is, they know the basics, but despite their efforts they cannot relate this basic information to anything they already know.

The above case exemplifies the second kind of problem which can exist when students are unable to apply learned information to a new situation. In this type of situation, the students have mastered the basic information and have been encouraged to apply it. The problem is that they are unsuccessful in the application. In contrast, where poor cognitive habits are the problem, the students have mastered the basic information but have not been asked to apply it to new situations.

In Chapter 5 we noted that this failure to understand resulted from the inability to relate newly learned information to previously established knowledge structures. This inability could become apparent when, for example, a search of long-term memory failed to locate any related information. The student is then faced with a situation where the only way to learn the material is to memorize it for recall. The information is thus being learned in a form that is not useful in solving novel problems.

8. Return for a moment to Question 7. What specific aspects of the case identify it as a problem involving a failure to understand rather than a problem of poor cognitive habits?

_____
_____
_____
_____
_____
- - - - - - - - - - - - - - - -

A problem involving poor cognitive habits is characterized by mastery of basic material, a lack of opportunity to apply the learned information to new situations, and an inability to apply the information when necessary. In contrast, inability to understand is characterized by mastery of basic material, ample opportunity to apply that information to new situations, and failure to respond successfully to the application problems.

The case in Question 7 had these later three characteristics. The students have done well on the recall questions (indicating mastery of the basic material), they frequently receive exposure to application questions (opportunity to apply the material), but they are unable to respond correctly to those questions requiring application of the material to new situations.

DESIGNING COGNITIVE LEARNING THEORY APPROACHES TO EDUCATIONAL PROBLEMS

Now that we have analyzed the two kinds of problems involved, let's discuss how to design a Cognitive Learning Theory approach to an identified problem.

Designing an approach to an educational problem based on Cognitive Learning Theory is more difficult than designing an approach based on applied Operant Learning Theory or Associative Learning Theory. Cognitive Learning Theory requires far more creative effort on the teacher's part than do the other two theories. We do not wish to imply that approaches based on the other two theories are easy to generate. Certainly numerous steps and attention to detail are required to develop approaches based on Associative Learning Theory and applied Operant Learning Theory. However, the procedure for these latter two approaches is well worked out, and, if a teacher carefully follows the specified steps, a useful set of instructional procedures will most likely result. But the case is different with Cognitive Learning Theory. In reality, no well-defined steps may be followed when generating a Cognitive Learning Theory approach to an educational problem. Instead, the teacher must rely heavily on educational intuition and knowledge of the world in developing viable Cognitive Learning Theory procedures.'

To clarify this problem, let's review what a teacher must do when faced with an educational problem involving poor cognitive habits or failure of understanding.

REVIEW

9. What should a teacher do when students cannot apply learned information, and the problem is poor cognitive habits?

_____

_____

- - - - - - - - - - - - - - - - - - - -

Give the students ample opportunity to apply learned information.

10. What should a teacher do when students cannot apply learned information and the problem is a failure to understand? (If you aren't sure, review pages 121-124 in Chapter 5.)

_____

_____

_____

- - - - - - - - - - - - - - - - -

The teacher should present the material so that the conceptual relationship between the new and the previously learned material is clear and explicit. Making these relationships explicit allows the student to integrate the material into previously established knowledge structures (thereby assuring understanding) and guards against rote learning.

At first glance these solutions appear fairly straightforward. But they are difficult to implement. To recommend the generation of application questions to accompany recall questions is one thing; to actually generate effective application questions is quite another. Similarly, to suggest that teaching should involve a process of systematically relating new information to old is easy to do, but to specify how the relationship should be established is often more difficult.

The development of effective application questions and strategies for relating new information to old, both require a truly creative effort from the teacher. No list of carefully worked-out steps to follow exists, only some common-sense rules of thumb. While these common-sense rules can provide some initial direction, they do not necessarily lead to the development of effective instructional materials and techniques. The quality of the materials and techniques will depend upon the effort and creativity of the individual teacher.

In the following pages we will discuss these rules of thumb and give you some practice in using them—as well as your own intuition and creativity—to develop application questions and instructional strategies. We will first consider how to generate application questions.

When generating application questions, the rule of thumb is to generate the questions in areas which are inherently interesting to the students. For example, assume you are teaching the metric system to a class of high school students. You could ask application questions such as, "How many liters are there in two gallons?" or "How many kilometers in three miles?" However, these application questions are unlikely to have much inherent interest for the students. Instead, you could ask questions like, "Would you rather have a case of half-quart cans of cola, or a case of liter bottles of cola?" or "If one car gets nine kilometers per liter of fuel, and another car gets twenty-six miles per gallon of fuel, which car is most economical?" The subject matter in these questions is more likely to hold some inherent interest for the students.

Consistent use of questions from inherently interesting areas can greatly reduce the problem of motivating students.

———————————————————————

11. Assume you are teaching an elementary school mathematics class in which you are studying percentages. What application questions involving percentages can you think of which might have some inherent interest for your students?

_____

_____

_____

_____

_____

- - - - - - - - - - - - - - - - - -

Many possibilities exist for good application question. Some that we thought of are as follows:

a. Computing batting averages for baseball players.
b. Determining the portions of ingredients which go into recipes when cooking for a larger or smaller number of people than the recipe calls for.
c. Calculating the interest earned on a savings account.
d. Calculating the percentage of the students in the class who have blond hair (or any other obvious characteristic).
e. Estimating the fairness of a tossed coin.

Note that some of these questions require other skills or knowlege. Be sure all of your students have the necessary background.

———————————————————————

Now suppose the teacher has generated application questions to accompany recall questions, and the students can correctly answer the recall questions but not the application questions. This problem involves a failure to understand reflecting an inability to relate the new material to previously learned material. As we have discussed, in this situation, the teacher should present the new information so that it is easily related to previously learned material, especially through analogies that make the relationships explicit. When generating analogies as an aid to understanding newly presented material, the rule of thumb is to base the analogy on information which is common to all of the students. For example, let's assume you were explaining to your students how a hydroelectric turbine (such as those found in hydroelectric plants) generates electricity. As an analogy, you tell your students that hydroelectric turbines work on the same principles as do the electric motors found in many household appliances. The chances are that you have not assisted the understanding process very much by using this analogy. Few students are likely to understand

electric motors any better than they understand hydroelectric turbines. If anything, the students are likely to be more confused than they were before. You
have presented them with two events they do not understand rather than just one!

Instead of the electric motor analogy, you should base your explanation on
knowledge which is almost certainly shared by all of the students. For example,
virtually all of the students have observed how a magnet either attracts or
repels (depending on the polar relationships) metallic substances. You could
use this experience to explain the operation of a hydroelectric turbine by pointing out that magnets also attract and repel free-floating electrons in a conducting material such as copper. When the magnet (propelled by water flow) is
moved back and forth through a coil of wire, the result is a current flow (of
moving electrons) which surges back and forth through the wire.

Below are several examples in which you should generate your own analogies to assist in the learning process.

12. Let's start with a fairly simple example. Assume that you were teaching
    your students about the operation of the human nervous system, and you
    were discussing how a message is sent from the brain to the muscles.
    What analogy can you think of which might aid your students in understand-
    ing the neural transmission process?

    _____

    _____

    _____

    _____

    _____

- - - - - - - - - - - - - - - - - - - -

    You could point out that the process of sending a message from the brain
    to the muscles is analogous to transmitting an electrical signal along a
    wire. In this analogy, the neurons of the nervous system are analogous to
    a conducting wire, and the nervous impulses are analogous to a surge of
    electricity being passed through the wire. Incidently, this analogy turns
    out to be particularly apt. The transmission of a message through the
    nervous system involves the transmission of an electrical potential.

13. Now let's try a more difficult example. Assume you were teaching your
    students about the homing instinct in salmon. As you are probably aware,
    salmon are spawned in continental rivers and then swim down the rivers
    to the ocean, where they live until they reach sexual maturity. Upon reach-
    ing maturity they return to the river of their birth, where they swim up-
    stream, deposit their eggs, and then die. The next generation hatches
    from the eggs, and the cycle begins again. Scientists were puzzled for
    many years as to how the salmon find their "home river." In the past few
    years they have discovered that each river has a unique mix of chemicals

(resulting from the leaching of minerals and the like) which gives that river a characteristic smell. The salmon has a remarkably sensitive olfactory system; when a salmon hatches, it stores the smell of the river in memory (this process is sometimes called imprinting). The salmon then swims down to the ocean and, upon reaching sexual maturity, begins to search for a water source having the same smell as the smell stored in memory. Upon finding the appropriate smell, the salmon simply follows the trail back to its original source.

If you wanted to explain the above information to your students, how would you do it so that you could be fairly sure that they understood the whole process?

_____

_____

_____

_____

_____

_____

_____

_____

- - - - - - - - - - - - - - - - - - -

Many methods of explanation would be equally effective. One we might try is as follows: We would first explain the nature of the problem to the students. That is, we would tell them that the salmon hatch, swim downriver to the ocean, stay there for several years, and then return to the same river to spawn. Then we would pose the question, "How do the salmon know which river to return to?"

We would then tell the students to imagine they grew up in a home where every Wednesday Mother baked apple pies. Each Wednesday, you could smell the pies baking and cooling (Mother put them on the windowsill to cool), and you could hardly wait for afternoon to roll around so that you could have a piece. One Wednesday you wandered out of the yard and start-started walking down the street. After walking for some time and making several turns, you decided to head back home, but you discovered you were lost! You walked and walked, but nothing seemed familiar. Just as the tears were coming to your eyes, your nose picked up a familiar aroma. Mother's apple pie! You began walking, always making sure that the aroma from the pies continued to get stronger, and you soon found yourself below the window where those beautiful pies sat on the sill.

After telling the story, we would point out how the lost child's dilemma is similar to that of the salmon, and how the salmon solves the dilemma in essentially the same way the child did.

Some of you may think that our story is fanciful and childish. Perhaps it is. However, our guess would be that students hearing the story would remember for a very long time how salmon return to rivers to spawn. And insuring that students remember is, after all, what teaching is all about.

We have now covered all of the essential details of applying Cognitive Learning Theory. We have also completed our discussion of the principles and applications of the major learning theories. In Chapter 7, we will present a framework which can help us decide which of the three theories we have discussed is most useful for a particular educational problem.

ADDITIONAL READINGS

Silberman, M. L., Allender, J. S., and Yanoff, J. M. (eds.). The Psychology of Open Teaching and Learning: An Inquiry Approach. Boston: Little, Brown and Company, 1972.

Snelbecker, G. E. Learning Theory, Instructional Theory, and Psychoeducational Design. New York: McGraw-Hill, 1974.

SELF-TEST

This self-test is designed to show you whether or not you have mastered the objectives of Chapter 6. Answer each question to the best of your ability, based on what you learned in this chapter. Correct answers are given following the test.

1. Briefly describe two classroom situations where Cognitive Learning Theory could be applied.

   a. _____

   _____

   _____

   b. _____

   _____

   _____

2. In each situation below, check (✓) whether the students display a lack of cognitive effort or a lack of conceptual understanding.

Lack of Cognitive Effort	Lack of Conceptual Understanding	
____	____	a. Mr. Jones has found that his students have tried to memorize word lists in his French class but don't truly comprehend the words.
____	____	b. Mr. Smith teaches through an inductive process, where he tries to have his students understand all facets of the topics in his science class. They still have difficulty in making new applications of the science principles on major tests, however.
____	____	c. Ms. Green takes all of her test questions from the end-of-chapter quizzes, using paraphrased versions of the original questions. The students answer the questions appropriately on homework assignments but have difficulty with the paraphrased questions.

Lack of   Lack of
Cognitive   Conceptual
Effort   Understanding

____   ____   d. Ms. Simpson gives a little quiz once a
                                 week to insure that basic historical facts
                                 are learned. However, the students seem
                                 to have difficulty properly applying these
                                 facts to their twice-a-year projects.

3. Imagine a teaching situation to which Cognitive Learning Theory could be
    appropriately applied. Consider the topic, what the students do and do not
    know, and how you will apply Cognitive Learning Theory to solve the
    problem. State the problem and how you will solve it.

    _____

    _____

    _____

    _____

    _____

    _____

    _____

ANSWERS TO SELF-TEST

Compare your answers to the questions on the self-test with the answers given below. If all of your answers are correct, you are ready to go on to the next chapter. If you missed any questions, review the appropriate parts of the chapter before you go on.

1. Your situations should describe students who have mastered the basic skills, but are having difficulty applying these basic skills to new and different situations.

2.

	Lack of Cognitive Effort	Lack of Conceptual Understanding
a.	✓	
b.		✓
c.	✓	
d.		✓

3. No "correct" answer can be given for this question. In evaluating your response, check to see that you considered these factors:

   a. Was the problem one where students mastered basics but were having difficulty applying the basics to more advanced situations?

   b. Was the problem lack of cognitive effort or lack of conceptual understanding?

   c. Was your approach based on applying the information to a variety of new situations, or did you choose a "discovery learning" approach?

   d. Did you include the principles of Cognitive Learning Theory in your solution?

If your answer incorporated the above points, then you have mastered the basic ideas behind applying Cognitive Learning Theory. Your success will now depend upon your experience and creativity.

PART FOUR
Application of Learning Theories in Classroom Situations

CHAPTER SEVEN
A Framework for Analyzing Problems and Applying Theory

In the previous chapters, we discussed three major learning theories and described how they could be applied to educational problems. We noted that each theory was uniquely suited for a particular kind of educational problem. But we have not taken into account the complexities of the actual classroom. A given classroom rarely contains only behavior-management problems or lack-of-basic-skills problems. A given classroom, or even an individual student, is much more likely to exhibit simultaneously all three of the types of problems we have described.

Given the complexities of the actual classroom, we must also discuss a procedure for analyzing the types of problems and deciding which learning theory would be most applicable to the identified problem. This chapter presents an integrated framework which can be used as a tool for analyzing educational problems and deciding upon an approach for solving the problem.

This chapter is divided into several sections. The first section will review the principles and application procedures for each of the learning theories we have discussed. The second section will present a framework for viewing educational problems and procedures for using that framework. The third section will present several case studies to give you practice in using the framework to analyze classroom problems.

Upon completion of this chapter, you will be able to:

Use the framework we have provided to analyze a series of case studies. This analysis will include: (1) determination of the nature of the problem or problems presented in the case studies, and (2) selection of the appropriate learning theory approach to apply to each problem.

REVIEW OF LEARNING THEORIES

Operant Learning Theory. Operant Learning Theory is based on the premise that the behavior of organisms is controlled by stimulus events occurring in the environment and environmental consequences which follow behavioral responses to those events. Thus, in the presence of a particular stimulus event, a response will tend to increase in frequency if the response is followed by reinforcement.

In education, Operant Learning Theory is most useful when the problem involves an easily observable behavioral action. Operant Learning Theory is, for example, a useful approach for problems involving disruptive classroom behavior, inattentiveness to instructional activities, or isolation from the classroom society. Operant Learning Theory is less useful in making decision about how most appropriately to present instructional materials. For example if the problem involves issues such as the most appropriate way to present the atomic theory of matter or the best way to remediate a particular reading problem, Operant Learning Theory provides us with few guidelines for proceeding. The Operant Learning Theory approach is outlined below.

Operant Learning Theory

Problem to be Solved	Steps
1. Disruptive classroom behavior	1. State the goal.
2. Inattentiveness	2. Identify target behavior for modification.
3. Isolation from classroom society	3. Choose the behavior modification approach to be used.
	4. Explain the rules to the children.
	5. Systematically apply the rules.

Associative Learning Theory. Associative Learning Theory is based on the premise that memory consists of representations of stimulus and response events joined together by an associative bond. These associative connections between stimulus and response events are formed when the stimulus and response events occur contiguously in the environment. Thus one distinction between Operant Learning Theory and Associative Learning Theory is in the importance of the consequences (for example, reinforcement or punishment) following a response. Operant Learning Theory maintains that these consequences are critical to learning. Associative Learning Theory maintains that the mere occurrence of a stimulus and response event together is sufficient to produce learning.

In education, Associative Learning Theory is most useful when applied to designing an instructional program for students lacking well-defined basic skills. For example, students who lack basic skills in reading or mathematics often can be helped by using an instructional procedure based upon Associative Learning Theory. Associative Learning Theory is not particularly useful when the educational problem involves overt student behaviors (or lack of behaviors) or complex educational skills. The Associative Learning Theory approach is outlined on the next page.

Associative Learning Theory

Problem to be Solved	Steps
1. Lack of basic skills and knowledge	1. Identify the terminal skill which is the goal of the instruction.
	2. Identify the skill level the student has attained before beginning the instruction.
	3. Break the terminal skill into the subskills and determine the sequence in which the subskills must be performed.
	4. Design instruction so that the subskills are presented and acquired in the appropriate sequence. Make sure the instruction is presented so as to maximize acquisition and retention of the skills or knowledge.

Cognitive Learning Theory. Cognitive Learning Theory, as outlined below, is based on the premise that the learner is an active participant in the learning process. According to this theory, the organism actively perceives, encodes, stores, and sometimes even alters the stimulus event being experienced. This view of the learner as an active participant in the learning process differs from that of Associative and Operant Learning Theory, in which the learner is viewed as a passive recorder of stimulus and response events.

Cognitive Learning Theory divides the learning process into a number of stages. The stimulus event from the outside world must be perceived, encoded, and matched, if possible, with information already existing in memory. The

Cognitive Learning Theory

Problem to be Solved	Steps
1. Skills and information to be mastered so that they may be applied to novel situations	1. Assess student entering skills and knowledge to assure that necessary basic information has been mastered.
	2. Provide students with ample opportunity to apply information to novel problems and situations.
	3. Systematically relate new information to previously learned information.

educational applications of Cognitive Learning Theory center on ways of facilitating the activity at the various stages.

Cognitive Learning Theory is most applicable to educational problems involving complex learning. It provides some guidelines for facilitating the acquisition of complex material such as concepts and principles, and it suggests ways in which students might acquire "learning to learn" skills. Cognitive Learning Theory is not particularly useful with problems involving overt student behaviors or the acquisition of basic skills.

A FRAMEWORK FOR ANALYZING CLASSROOM PROBLEMS

Now let's look at the framework for analyzing classroom problems. This framework is based on the assumption that one of the basic purposes of education is to help students acquire academic skills and knowledge in a form most useful for dealing with real-world problems and experiences. In other words, the skills and knowledge acquired in the classroom should be applicable to real-world events. Cognitive Learning Theory is directed to precisely this goal. As we learned in Chapters 5 and 6, teachers can guide their students toward this goal by providing them with ample opportunity to apply learned information to new situations; teachers can also facilitate the understanding process by relating new information to previously learned information.

A precondition for learning material in the most usable form, however, is that the students must have mastered the basic skills and knowledge that enable them to apply learned information to new situations. For example, we could not expect a student to be able to determine in square feet the area of a rug if the student could not compute the area of a rectangle. Associative Learning Theory, the topic of Chapters 3 and 4, provides guidelines for developing instructional procedures designed to remedy problems involving a lack of basic skills.

However, a precondition for mastering basic academic skills and knowledge is that students must perform behaviors which lead to the acquisition of the necessary academic material. That is, they must pay attention to presented instruction, study and read when appropriate, and practice newly presented material in order to master it. In addition, they should not frequently engage in behaviors which disrupt their own learning activities or those of others around them. This precondition involves observable student behavior, which is the focus of applied Operant Learning Theory, presented in Chapters 1 and 2.

Thus, students must engage in appropriate academic behaviors before they can master basic skills and knowledge, and they must master basic skills and knowledge before they can apply the information to novel situations. These dependency relationships allow us to construct a decision checklist which can be used to diagnose the nature of the educational problems existing in a classroom (or with an individual student) and to decide upon the appropriate learning theory approach to use.

1. Below we present a partially filled-in decision checklist. Your task is to complete the checklist.

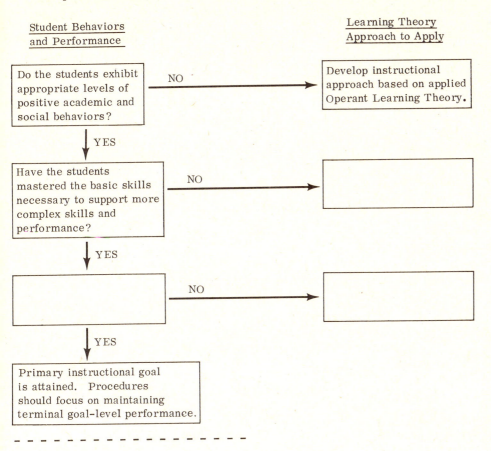

Student Behaviors and Performance — Learning Theory Approach to Apply

Do the students exhibit appropriate levels of positive academic and social behaviors? — NO → Develop instructional approach based on applied Operant Learning Theory.

↓ YES

Have the students mastered the basic skills necessary to support more complex skills and performance? — NO → [blank]

↓ YES

[blank] — NO → [blank]

↓ YES

Primary instructional goal is attained. Procedures should focus on maintaining terminal goal-level performance.

- - - - - - - - - - - - - - - -

Your completed checklist should be similar to the one on the following page.

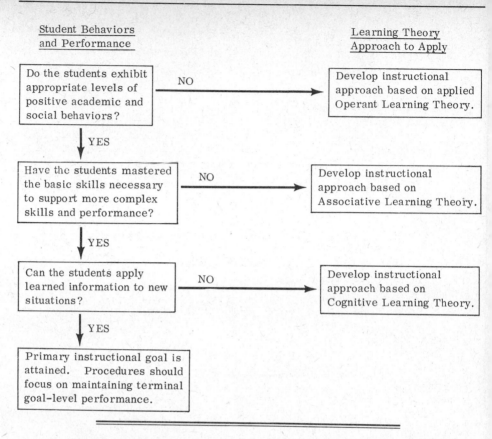

Student Behaviors and Performance / Learning Theory Approach to Apply

Do the students exhibit appropriate levels of positive academic and social behaviors? — NO → Develop instructional approach based on applied Operant Learning Theory.

↓ YES

Have the students mastered the basic skills necessary to support more complex skills and performance? — NO → Develop instructional approach based on Associative Learning Theory.

↓ YES

Can the students apply learned information to new situations? — NO → Develop instructional approach based on Cognitive Learning Theory.

↓ YES

Primary instructional goal is attained. Procedures should focus on maintaining terminal goal-level performance.

The above checklist can be used in a variety of ways. You could use the checklist to obtain a fairly general assessment of an entire class of students. Or, even better, you could use the checklist with individual students. For example, the checklist could be used to determine what type of learning program would be best for a given student and to chart the progress made by that student. As an example of this type of usage, analyze the situation below.

Imagine you were teaching an elementary-level mathematics class, and your major task for the first several weeks of the school year was to cover subtraction of whole numbers, subtraction of decimals, and subtraction of fractions. Before the beginning of the school year, you made up a checklist form (Table 2). After school was in session for several weeks, you rated each of your students on their classroom behaviors, mastery of basic skills, and ability to apply learned information to new problems, as indicated on the form on the following page.

Table 2. Student Checklist

Student's Name	Whole numbers			Decimals			Fractions		
	Sat. acad. & soc. behav.[1]	Sat. basic skills[2]	Sat. application[3]	Sat. acad. & soc. behav.	Sat. basic skills	Sat. application	Sat. acad. & soc. behav.	Sat. basic skills	Sat. application
Sarah Towell	✓	✓			✓	✓	✓	✓	
Bill Fames	✓	✓	✓	✓	✓	✓	✓	✓	
Cliff Conold	✓			✓	✓		✓	✓	
Molly Fermi	✓			✓	✓	✓	✓	✓	
Dolly Jolly				✓			✓	✓	
Jack Cates	✓	✓	✓	✓	✓	✓	✓	✓	
Marcy Jerkins	✓			✓	✓		✓	✓	
Greg Lamey				✓	✓		✓	✓	
Michael Parten	✓	✓		✓	✓	✓	✓	✓	
Kent Bohnsen							✓	✓	

[1]Satisfactory academic and social behaviors
[2]Satisfactory basic skills
[3]Satisfactory application of learned skills to new situations

2. Based on the data given in Table 2, decide which learning theory approach you would take with each student.

Sarah   _____

Bill   _____

Cliff   _____

Molly   _____

Dolly   _____

Jack   _____

Marcy   _____

Greg   _____

Michael _____

Kent   _____

Sarah: Sarah's classroom behavior is satisfactory and her mastery of basic skills is adequate. Cognitive Learning Theory could be used to increase application ability.

Bill: Bill's behavior is satisfactory in all three of the checklist categories. Maintenance procedures should continue.

Cliff: Cliff's classroom behavior is satisfactory, but he lacks mastery of basic skills. Associative Learning Theory is called for.

Molly: Molly's classroom behavior is satisfactory, but she lacks mastery of basic skills. Associative Learning Theory is called for.

Dolly: Dolly has classroom behavior problems. Start with applied Operant Learning Theory.

Jack: Jack is satisfactory in all three of the checklist categories. No special procedures are called for.

Marcy: Marcy is satisfactory in classroom behavior, but she lacks basic skills. Associative Learning Theory is called for.

Greg: Greg has classroom behavior problems. Start with applied Operant Learning Theory.

Michael: Michael has satisfactory classroom behavior, and he has attained adequate mastery of basic skills. He needs to build skills in applying learned information. Cognitive Learning Theory is called for.

Kent: Kent has unsatisfactory classroom behavior. Start with applied Operant Learning Theory.

Let's assume that time has passed, and you have developed programs for each of your students based on your analysis of their behavioral and performance competencies. You are teaching the section on fractions, and you have just completed your latest checklist ratings. They appear in Table 3.

You should notice several facts revealed in Table 3. First, the checklist can be used to chart the progress of individual students. Dolly, Greg, and Kent had unsatisfactory levels of classroom behaviors in the section on subtraction of whole numbers. By the time the rating was made on subtraction of decimals, Dolly and Greg had improved to the point where their academic and social behaviors were rated as satisfactory. Kent did not show improvement by the decimal rating period. However, when the fractions rating was made his behavior had improved to the point that it was satisfactory. Notice also that the students who had been deficient in basic skills (Cliff, Molly, and Marcy) were exhibiting satisfactory mastery of basic skills when the rating on fractions was completed.

Table 3. Student Checklist During Fraction Work

| Student's Name | Subject: Subtraction | | | | | | | | |
| | Whole numbers | | | Decimals | | | Fractions | | |
	Sat. acad. & soc. behav.[1]	Sat. basic skills[2]	Sat. application[3]	Sat. acad. & soc. behav.	Sat. basic skills	Sat. application	Sat. acad. & soc. behav.	Sat. basic skills	Sat. application
Sarah Towell	✓	✓							
Bill Fames	✓	✓	✓						
Cliff Conold	✓								
Molly Fermi	✓								
Dolly Jolly									
Jack Cates	✓	✓	✓						
Marcy Jerkins	✓								
Greg Lamey									
Michael Parten	✓	✓							
Kent Bohnsen									

[1] Satisfactory academic and social behaviors
[2] Satisfactory basic skills
[3] Satisfactory application of learned skills to new situations

3. One striking aspect of the data on fractions in Table 3 is that none of the students are demonstrating satisfactory ability to apply learned information to new situations. Thinking back to Chapter 5, what would be your guess as to why they are not?

_____

_____

_____

_____

- - - - - - - - - - - - - - - - - - -

Two possible reasons are likely for the students' inability to apply learned information to new situations. First, the students may not have been given the opportunity to practice applying learned information to new situations. If the students have had ample practice in applying learned information and are still unable to do so, then the most likely explanation is that they lack a basic conceptual understanding of the material.

4. If you decide that the problem does involve a lack of conceptual understanding, what do you do?

_____

_____

_____

_____

- - - - - - - - - - - - - - - - - - -

Develop teaching procedures which would facilitate integration of the new material into existing knowlege structure. "Teaching by analogy" techniques, for example, would systematically relate the new information to information the student already knows.

═══════════════════════════════════

CASE STUDIES: PRACTICE IN ANALYZING CLASSROOM PROBLEMS

In this section we will present three case studies. The first two case studies will be fairly short. We will ask you to diagnose the nature of the problem in these two studies and to select an appropriate learning theory approach for it. The third case study will be somewhat longer. In addition to diagnosing the problem and selecting the appropriate learning theory approach, we will ask you to carry out the preliminary steps of the selected approach.

Case Study 1. Ms. Abigail Adams has just been assigned to teach a ninth grade civics class. One of the most important things she wants to accomplish during the semester is to familiarize her students with the documents which form the foundation of the government of the United States. More specifically, she wants her students to be able to identify the purpose, general contents, and modern-day importance of the Declaration of Independence, the Bill of Rights, and the Constitution of the United States. During the first week of class, she gave all of her students the following homework assignment. For each of the documents named above, they were to answer these questions:

1. Why was the document written?
2. What were some of the major features of the document?
3. Why is the document important to us today?

One week later she sat down and made the following notes based on the answers the students wrote to her questions and on her observations of their classroom behavior since the beginning of the semester.

Bill Foomey:	Bill gave the longest answer of any of the students. He wrote that the purpose of the Declaration of Independence was to separate the United States from Great Britain and Canada and that the purpose of the Bill of Rights and the Constitution was to get rid of the King of the United States and to form a democratically governed nation. He went on to note that these documents resulted in a war between the United States on one side and Great Britain and Canada on the other. He indicated that the modern-day importance of the documents derived from the fact that the United States won the war and conquered the territory we now know as New England. If the war had not been fought and won, the United States would be much smaller than it currently is.

Bill appears to work hard in school, and he is attentive and well behaved in class. He seems to have some difficulty in reading, and his writing is characterized by more grammar, punctuation, and spelling errors than a ninth grader should show.

Sally Tonfron:	Sally did not hand in answers to the questions. Her classroom behavior thus far is troublesome. Whenever she is asked a question, she manages to come up with a "smart-alecky" answer that has the class in stiches. Already I have developed the tendency not to ask her questions (is she modifying my behavior?). Sally is obviously very clever and could probably do well if she tried.
Herford Bovine:	Herford, who is nicknamed "Cud" by his classmates, wrote that the basic purpose of the Declaration of Independence was to state the moral and philosophical basis for the separation of the United States from Great Britain. The document asserted that men are born with certain "inalienable rights" and that the relationship which existed at the time between the United States and Britain did not allow the expression of those rights. He further wrote that the modern importance of the Declaration of Independence is largely symbolic, in that it serves as a statement of our raison d'être. Herford wrote that the purpose of our Bill of Rights and the Constitution was to specify the form of the new government and to specify those individual rights which were outside of the realm of government intervention. He went on to say that the modern-day importance of these documents resided in the fact that they served as standards against which any modern-day governmental change or law could be tested.

Herford's classroom behavior is characterized best by the term "isolate." He is frequently the object of classroom pranks and jokes (witness the nickname "Cud' rarely interacts with other students in the class, and seems to have few close friends outside of the class-room.

---

5. Using the above descriptions of the three students, rate each student with respect to the following three categories of behaviors and skills (or knowledge):

 1. Is the classroom behavior displayed by the student satisfactory?
 2. Does the student exhibit mastery of basic skills and knowledge which would serve as the foundation for more complex learning?
 3. Can the student apply mastered skills and knowledge to new situations?

- - - - - - - - - - - - - - - - - - -

Your answers should be similar to those below:

Bill Foomey: Classroom behavior: satisfactory. Bill is attentive in class, works hard, and completes work when it is due.

Basic skills and knowledge: unsatisfactory. Bill is deficient in several basic skills; he reads poorly and is deficient in writing skills. In addition, his mastery of basic facts about the history of the United States leaves much to be desired. His misinformation results in an inability to formulate plausible implications of past events for today's society.

Ability to apply learned information: unsatisfactory. The implications Bill has suggested are off the mark, probably due to his lack of basic knowledge.

Sally Tonfron: Classroom behavior: unsatisfactory. Sally is a "class-room clown" who devotes more time to answering her peers than she does to doing her work.

Basic skills and knowledge: probably unsatisfactory. Sally's level of appropriate classroom behavior is so low that her level of basic skill and knowledge mastery cannot be determined. Definitive evidence in this area will have to await appropriate levels of classroom behavior.

Ability to apply learned information: probably unsatisfactory. Again, a definitive classification could be made only after appropriate levels of classroom behavior had been established.

Herford Bovine: Classroom behavior: unsatisfactory. Herford is an interesting student in that his <u>academic</u> classroom behavior is perfectly satisfactory. However, his <u>social</u> classroom behavior is not. Under the assumption that schools have a responsibility in the social, as well as the academic, area, a program should be developed which would attempt to improve Herford's social skills.

Basic skills and knowledge and ability to apply learned information: satisfactory; in fact, exceptional.

The students discussed in Case Study 1 illustrate an important point regarding the use of the decision framework we presented earlier in this chapter. We suggested that behaviors, skills, and knowledge could be viewed as a hierarchy, where the achievement of one goal in the hierarchy was dependent upon having already achieved goals lower in the hierarchy. That is, the ability to apply learned information to new situations depends upon mastery of basic skills and knowledge, and mastery of basic skills and knowledge depends upon appropriate levels of academic and classroom behaviors. These dependency relationships hold when we are focusing only on academically related behaviors and skills, but not necessarily when the focus is on social skills. Herford, one of the boys in Case Study 1, is an example of a student who is satisfactory in upper-level academic goals but unsatisfactory in lower-level social behaviors.

6. Based on your analysis of the type of problem present for each student in Case Study 1, what learning theory approach would you use for each?

Bill: _____

_____

Sally: _____

_____

Herford: _____

_____

Bill: An Associative Learning Theory approach designed to improve basic skills and knowledge.

Sally: An applied Operant Learning Theory approach designed to attain satisfactory levels of appropriate classroom behavior.

Herford: An applied Operant Learning Theory approach designed to attain satisfactory levels of appropriate social behavior.

Case Study 2. Mr. Brownian teaches a fourth grade class in general science. He has been teaching for several years. Recently he has made a majo change in his approach to teaching. He has decided to try a more "open" approach in which the majority of work performed by the students consists of independent projects completed either by individual students or by groups of students. Mr. Brownian's major goal for the current teaching period is for his students to acquire a basic understanding of the changes which occur in matter as it moves from one state to another (from a solid to a liquid, from a liquid to a gas, and so on). During the semester, Mr. Brownian has worked with his students in setting up independent study projects, and he has also collected some data on the kinds of activities his students are engaged in during science class. For example, he has recorded that his students were involved in some sort of social interaction during 75 percent of the intervals at which he observed them and that they were involved in behaviors contrary to the classroom rules during 15 percent of the observation periods.

Mr. Brownian wanted to conduct an evaluation of his teaching experiment. As part of the process, he administered a test on which he asked the following kinds of questions: (1) What are the three states in which matter can exist? (2) Can all forms of matter exist in more than one state? (3) Which is warmest, liquid oxygen or gaseous oxygen? (4) If you filled a balloon with steam and then left it for an hour at room temperature (a) what would the balloon look like after an hour? (b) would the balloon weigh more just after you filled it, or after you waited the hour? (5) Why do we fill our automobile tires with air rather than with steam? (6) If you could collect a dime for every molecule of water, would you rather have a cubic centimeter of ice, or a cubic centimeter of water?

Table 4 summarizes the performance of each of the class members on Mr. Brownian's test.

Table 4. Summary of Test Performance

Student's Name	Questions 1-3 Correct	Questions 4-6 Correct
Mary	Yes	Yes
Sandra	Yes	No
Timothy	No	No
Jean	Yes	Yes

Student's Name	Questions 1–3 Correct	Questions 4–6 Correct
Riley	No	No
Phillip	Yes	Yes
Glen	Yes	Yes
Paula	Yes	Yes
Clifford	Yes	No
Jack	No	No

7. Since Mr. Brownian wants an assessment of whether his new approach is viable for an entire class of students, our questions will consider the class as a unit. First, are the students exhibiting appropriate levels of classroom behavior? Explain.

_____

_____

_____

- - - - - - - - - - - - - - - -

Yes. Behavior contrary to classroom rules is occurring at about 15 percent of the observation intervals, which is probably a satisfactory level. In addition, since Mr. Brownian is using an approach which emphasizes group work, he expects a high level of social interaction in his classroom. The 75 percent level indicates that the approach is encouraging social interchange.

8. Are the students in Mr. Brownian's class demonstrating a satisfactory level of basic skill and knowledge mastery? Why, or why not?

_____

_____

_____

- - - - - - - - - - - - - - - -

This question is actually a very tough one, and we hope you had some difficulty in answering it. First, you should have noticed that Questions 1–3 were asking for direct recall of learned information. In addition, you should have noticed that 70 percent (7 out of 10) of the students answered these questions correctly. Is 70 percent a satisfactory level of mastery? The answer to this question depends on the goals that the individual teacher has set. Some teachers would be happy if 70 percent of the students mastered the information, and some would be disappointed. Our bias is to lean toward disappointment and to develop procedures which would result in mastery for those nonmastery students.

9. Have the students in Mr. Brownian's class mastered the material to the point where they can apply it to new situations? Why, or why not?

_____

_____

_____

_____

- - - - - - - - - - - - - - - - - - -

The students' performance on Questions 4-6 provides the relevant data for answering this question. Again, the answer to the question depends on the goals the teacher has set. Fifty percent of the students answered questions 4-6 correctly, and some teachers would take this figure as evidence that the teaching approach being used resulted in satisfactory levels of student learning. However, our bias is again to strive for higher levels of success.

10. Suppose that Mr. Brownian was not satisfied by the performance exhibited by his students. What would you recommend that he do? Provide a separate recommendation for each of the following students:

Sandra: _____

Timothy: _____

Riley: _____

Clifford: _____

Jack: _____

- - - - - - - - - - - - - - - - - - -

Sandra: Sandra exhibits mastery of basic knowledge, but she is unable to apply her knowledge to new situations. A Cognitive Learning Theory approach should be developed to guide her toward this goal.

Timothy: Timothy has not mastered the basic knowledge tested in Questions 1-3, and he cannot apply learned information as tested by Questions 4-6. As a first step, an Associative Learning Theory approach should be developed to build up his basic knowledge.

Riley: Riley is in the same position as Timothy, and the recommendation should be the same.

Clifford: Your recommendation for Clifford should be the same as that for Sandra.

Jack: Your recommendation should be the same as that for Timothy and Riley.

Case Study 3. Ms. Wilson is a second grade teacher in a small town in the Midwest. One of her major teaching goals is to improve the reading competencies of her students. At the beginning of the school year, she gave her class a reading test she had developed to assess basic reading skills such as letter recognition, word recognition, knowledge of vocabulary, and word blending. In addition, the test was designed to assess the higher-level goal of reading comprehension. In addition to administering the reading test, Ms. Wilson also kept informal notes on the classroom behaviors of her students.

Based on the data mentioned above, Ms. Wilson completed a checklist of behaviors and skills for each of her pupils. The checklist is presented in Table 5.

Table 5. Behavior and Skills Checklist

Student's Name	Satisfactory Classroom Behavior	Satisfactory Basic Skills	Satisfactory Reading Comprehension
Larry Schmidt	Yes	Yes	No
Helen Gurney	Yes	Yes	No
Harry Jolson	No	No	No
Susan Blake	Yes	Yes	Yes
Jimmy Brown	Yes	Yes	Yes
Carla Beck	No	No	No
Greg Toland	Yes	Yes	No
Judy Grant	Yes	Yes	Yes
Ted Carlton	Yes	Yes	Yes
Mickey Stanley	No	Yes	Yes

Ms. Wilson's notes on the three students who were rated as unsatisfactory in classroom behavior are listed below.

Harry Jolson: Harry is very popular with his fellow students and spends an excessive amount of time talking, moving about the class, shouting out comments about questions directed to other students, and disturbing other students when they are trying to work. Harry is also deficient in basic reading skills. He can recognize and label the letters of the alphabet, but he has difficulty in sounding out letters and blending the letters into sounds. Because of these difficulties, his reading comprehension is very poor.

Carla Beck: Carla is physically larger than her fellow classmates and she is rapidly becoming the classroom bully. She often verbally abuses other students in the class, and sometimes even hits them or throws objects at them. She seems to do these things largely to gain attention, and sometimes seems to wait until I'm watching before she bullies another student. Carla's reading problems are much the same as Harry's. She has considerable difficulty in sounding out letters and blending the sounds into words. Her reading comprehension is very poor.

Mickey Stanley: Mickey's behavior problem is social in nature. She is an excessively shy girl and seems very hesitant to interact with her fellow classmates. She goes outside at recess only at my insistence, preferring instead to stay inside and draw or read. Her reading skills are exceptional, in that she displays excellent mastery of both basic reading skills and reading comprehension.

The notes above provide a description of each of the students who were rated as unsatisfactory in classroom behavior and, in two of the three cases, on mastery of basic skills. Below are the notes that Ms. Wilson made on the remaining students who were rated as unsatisfactory on reading comprehension.

Larry Schmidt: Larry has mastered basic reading skills, but he has difficulty in fully comprehending and drawing implications from what he is reading. For example, the other day in class Larry read the sentence, "Mary gave the candy to her brother Jimmy." When I asked, "Who has the candy?" Larry's first response was, "I don't know." When I pressed him, he answered, "Larry."

Helen Gurney: Helen demonstrates good mastery of basic reading skills and she displays adequate comprehension of short declarative sentences. However, with longer sentences she begins to display some difficulties in understanding what she is reading. She seems almost to forget what she read in the early part of a sentence by the time she gets to the end of a sentence longer than four or five words.

Greg Toland: Greg's problem is very similar to Larry's. His reading performance seems to involve almost an automatic mouthing of words, without storing in memory the information he is reading. After he has finished reading a sentence, he is frequently unable to answer a question about what he has read.

11. We are now ready to begin to develop procedures for dealing with the problem in Ms. Wilson's class. What learning theory approach would you use with the three students who display behavior problems, and what is the first step to take in implementing the approach you have chosen?

_____

_____

_____

_____

- - - - - - - - - - - - - - - - - -

You should have chosen applied Operant Learning Theory. The first step in implementing this approach is to state the goal of the learning approach in behavioral terms.

12. Provide a behaviorally defined goal statement for each student who has behavioral problems.

Harry Jolson: _____

_____

Carla Beck: _____

_____

Mickey Stanley: _____

_____

- - - - - - - - - - - - - - - - - -

Your goal statement should contain two essential details. First, it should state a desired level of <u>inappropriate</u> <u>behavior</u> to be attained. And second, it should state a desired level of <u>appropriate</u> <u>behavior</u> to be attained. Our statements are presented below as examples.

Harry Jolson: The program goal is to reduce Harry's level of inappropriate classroom activity (for example, talking or disturbing others) to 15 percent of measured observation intervals and to increase his level of appropriate classroom activity (for example, working quietly and staying in his seat) to 80 percent of the appropriate observation intervals.

Carla Beck: The program goal for Carla is to reduce her frequency of abusive behaviors (for example, verbal abuse or hitting) to 0 percent of the observation intervals and to increase her frequency of cooperative social behaviors to 70 percent of the appropriate observation intervals.

Mickey Stanley: The program goal for Mickey is to reduce the frequency of her "isolate" behavior (for example, withdrawal from social contact and discouraging social approach) to 20 percent of the observation intervals and to increase the frequency of positive social contact to 60 percent of the appropriate observation intervals.

The behavioral levels mentioned above are fairly arbitrary. In an actual classroom setting, you should choose levels which you consider desirable.

13. Once you have established goals for your Operant Learning Theory approach, what is the next step in implementing the program?

_____

_____

_____

- -

The next step would be identifying target behaviors for modification. Several instances of possible target behaviors for the three students are mentioned in Answer 12.

Since Chapter 2 gave considerable practice in carrying out all of the steps in an applied Operant Learning Theory approach, we will not continue our analysis of the behavior problems in Ms. Wilson's class any further. However, some of you may wish to complete developing this approach on your own, for additional practice.

Let us assume that Ms. Wilson's approach to the behavior problems in her class has shown some immediate results and she is now ready to tackle the problem of lack of basic skills.

14. What learning theory approach would be used to build up the basic reading skills for Harry and Carla?

_____

_____

- -

Associative Learning Theory.

15. What is the first step in implementing an Associative Learning Theory approach designed to master basic reading skills for Harry and Carla?

_____

Complete this step for each student.

Harry: _____

_____

Carla: _____

_____

- - - - - - - - - - - - - - - - -

The first step in implementing an Associative Learning Theory approach to an educational problem is to specify the desired terminal skill. Since Harry and Carla are deficient in the same basic skills, one objective (or goal) will serve for both of them. Your objective should be stated in behavioral terms and should specify how you will determine if the objective has been attained. Our objective is: At the end of instruction, the student will be able to correctly sound out and blend together the letters for any of the words chosen at random from the appropriate grade-level text.

16. Ms. Wilson has administered a test to her students near the beginning of the semester. Would the results of this test be relevant to completing any of the remaining steps in an Associative Learning Theory approach for Harry and Carla? Explain.

_____

_____

- - - - - - - - - - - - - - - - -

Yes. The second step in developing an Associative Learning Theory approach is to assess the skill level attained by the student before the instruction. The results from Ms. Wilson's test could provide the data for this assessment.

We will now conclude our analysis of the basic skill problem in Ms. Wilson's class. If you want additional practice in developing an Associative Learning Theory approach, you may wish, on your own, to continue the analysis through the remaining steps.

We will now turn to the final problem present in Ms. Wilson's class: the inability to comprehend the material being read.

17. What learning theory approach would you recommend for dealing with the problem of lack of reading comprehension?

_____

_____

- - - - - - - - - - - - - - - - - -

We hope you said Cognitive Learning Theory.

Reading comprehension is a very good example of cognitive processing in learning. The material on a printed page must be perceived and translated into some internal representation; then, for comprehension to occur, this internal representation must make contact with previously stored knowledge. Failure to comprehend might be traced to any of several steps in this sequence of activities. The student's perceptual process could be faulty (if, for example reading problems were due to dyslexia), or the student might experience difficulty in the internal translation process (by failing to sound out words correctly, or the like) or in relating the incoming representation to information already stored in memory.

18. Based on the descriptions we have provided for each of the students having reading comprehension problems, identify the stage which is probably responsible for their reading comprehension difficulties.

Larry Schmidt: _____

_____

Helen Gurney: _____

_____

Harry Jolson: _____

_____

Carla Beck: _____

_____

Greg Toland: _____

_____

- - - - - - - - - - - - - - - - - -

Since all of the students are able to identify and label letters, the perceptual process is probably not at fault. Two of the students (Harry and Carla) have basic skills problems, which suggests that both are having difficulty translating perceived information into stable, accurate, internal representations. As noted previously, an Associative Learning Theory approach could be used to remedy this type of problem. The remaining students (Larry, Helen, and Greg) seem to be having difficulty in integrating incoming information into previously established knowledge structures.

19. Given that the problems being experienced by Larry, Helen, and Greg involve problems in integrating incoming information into previously established knowledge structure, Cognitive Learning Theory seems to be a viable approach for dealing with the problem. Using this approach, what would you recommend that Ms. Wilson do to increase reading comprehension performance for her students? Remember that failures in cognitive learning are generally due to either lack of practice in applying learned information to new situations (poor cognitive habits) or to an inability to comprehend in a meaningful way the information being learned.

_____

_____

_____

- - - - - - - - - - - - - - - - -

Ms. Wilson's students are probably having difficulty because they lack practice in relating incoming information to previously acquired information. Ms. Wilson could try to remedy this situation by frequently asking questions which require the application of the learned (or read) information to new situations. For example, she might ask questions which require the student to draw implications from the material being read.

Afterword

William James once wrote that the world must appear to be a "blooming-buzzing confusion" to a newborn child. This description probably aptly sums up the way a classroom appears to a new teacher on the first day of class. The teacher is faced with twenty to forty strangers, each with his or her own personality and behavior pecularities and each with a particular learning history and a special blend of skills and learning deficits. The teacher must try to understand each of these personalities and to guide them toward agreed-upon learning goals.

In many ways, a skillful teacher is similar to a skillful physician. The physician must consider carefully the complaints and symptoms of a given patient, diagnose the disorder the patient is experiencing, and prescribe a treatment which is designed to remedy the disorder. Similarly, a good teacher must consider carefully the behaviors, skills, and knowledge a student brings to the learning situation, decide what behavioral and learning goals the student should attain, and develop a plan of action which will move the student toward those goals.

The analogy between a physician's activities and a teacher's activities goes deeper than superficial similarities. The physician brings to the job a set of "tools" which greatly facilitates his or her ability to assist patients. For example, the physician can call upon modern drugs, complex medical technologies, and sophisticated surgical procedures. The skillful teacher also has a set of tools to use in accomplishing educational goals. Often, teachers have acquired these tools through experience. They learn by trial and error that material presented in one way may be difficult to learn, but, presented in another way, it will be easier to learn. They also learn by experience that an approach which is successful with one type of student may not be success-ful with a different type.

We strongly believe in the value of experience. Many "tools" that teachers use can be acquired only after long periods of trying, failing, and trying again. However, we also believe that valuable conceptual tools exist which can assist teachers in their jobs. Our purpose in writing this book has been to familiar-ize you with conceptual tools based on theories of human learning. We believe that a teacher who thoroughly understands the principles of learning theories and the procedures for translating these theories into practical approaches will have acquired a valuable tool to assist in solving many of the learning problems which arise in the classroom.

Index